MW01599885

Three Essays on Freedom

John W. Parsons

Three Essays on Freedom

Freedom is a Lonely Star

Freedom is a Two-Edged Sword

Doing Your Will

by

John Whiteside (Jack) Parsons

Edited with a Foreword by
Hymenaeus Beta

The Teitan Press
2008

Published in 2008 by
The Teitan Press
P.O. Box 2050
York Beach, ME 03910-2050 USA
www.teitanpress.com

Printed in the United States of America

First Edition

Limited to 418 Numbered Copies

This is copy No. *182*

ISBN 978-0-933429-11-6

Dustjacket photograph courtesy NASA/JPL-Caltech

Parsons texts and frontispiece photograph
©2008 The Cameron Parsons Foundation
Published by arrangement with Thelema Media LLC
www.cameron-parsons.org

Foreword ©2008 Ordo Templi Orientis

This paper meets the requirements of
ANSI/NISO Z39.48-1992 (Permanence of Paper)

Contents

Foreword

We have it in our power to begin the world over again.
Thomas Paine, *Common Sense*

THE LAST of the late Arthur C. Clarke's famous "three laws" states that "any sufficiently advanced technology is indistinguishable from magic." A corollary might be "any sufficiently mature magick manifests as technology." John Whiteside (Jack) Parsons (1914–1952) left his mark in both fields. Inextricably intertwined with these were his deep political convictions, set out in the essay "Freedom is a Lonely Star," recently brought to light by Keith Richmond and published here for the first time.

By the 20th century, technological innovations were no longer a handmaiden to war and politics; they had become an often unpredictable driving force in their own right that upset long-established balances of power. Those in power regarded the geniuses that discovered new technologies with mingled awe, veneration and fear.

Individual cases can shed light on this phenomenon. There were three notable one-man "technology transfers" of rocket and missile technology from one country to another in the post-WWII era and the early years of the Cold War. All are directly comparable; each was handled differently; only two came to fruition.

The best known is America's secret patriation of the ex-Nazi rocket scientist Wernher von Braun (1912–1977), whose V2 rockets had rained automated, pilotless death on England from the skies, opening a new chapter in warfare. Von Braun was relocated to Alabama, where he led the post-war rocket research program that culminated in America's strategic missile system as well as the Apollo moon program.

Less well known is the case of the Chinese rocket scientist Qian Xuesen (Tsien Hue-Shen, 1911–), for many years a close colleague of Jack Parsons at the lab that became the Jet Propulsion Laboratory. Qian earned his doctorate at the

California Institute of Technology and was later appointed Goddard Professor there. After his 1950 application for American citizenship, the FBI and INS investigated him for Communist sympathies, subjecting him to five years in an administrative limbo that was practically house arrest. He was deported to China in 1950, disgusted with America's xenophobic paranoia. Undersecretary of the Navy Daniel Kimball remarked "I'd rather see him shot than let him go. ... He's worth three to five divisions anyplace."[1]

He was worth much more, in retrospect—Qian brought China's intercontinental ballistic missile program to fruition, and led development of the rocket that made possible China's first manned space flight.[2] Kimball later reflected that "It was the stupidest thing this country ever did ... he was no more a Communist than I was and we forced him to go."[3]

The third one-man technology transfer was thwarted at the last minute—or rather on the last day—by the death of Jack Parsons at the age of thirty-seven.[4] He died on June 17, 1952—the day he was to leave the United States for good—in an explosion in his home laboratory. He and his wife Cameron were moving to Mexico, but this was temporary; their ultimate destination was the new state of Israel, where they hoped to raise a family free of the afflictions that they believed beset life in America.[5] Some of the best minds from around the world were gathering to build the new state of Israel; it promised a fresh start.

-----

1. In Lyle J. Goldstein, ed., with Andrew S. Erickson, *China's Nuclear Force Modernization (Newport Papers 22)* (Newport: Navy War College, 2005), p. 55; online at http://www.nwc.navy.mil/press/newportpapers/documents/22. pdf, accessed May 28, 2008.

2. See William L. Ryan and Sam Summerlin, *The China Cloud* (Boston: Little, Brown, 1967), and Iris Chang, *The Thread of the Silkworm* (New York: Basic Books, 1995; rpt. 1999).

3. In Bradley Perrett, "Qian Xuesen Laid Foundation for Space Rise in China," *Aviation Week and Space Technology* 168(1), pp. 57–61. Qian was named the journal's Person of the Year in 2008.

4. For Parsons' biography, see George Pendle, *Strange Angel: The Otherwordly Life of Rocket Scientist John Whiteside Parsons* (Orlando: Harcourt, 2005).

5. Cameron Parsons Kimmel, personal communication, 1986.

Parsons was tired, professionally frustrated and angry with America. His ties to Israel and his intellectual curiosity about socialism and communism had attracted the attention of the FBI; eventually, his military security clearance was revoked, effectively ending his career in rocket research. His bitterness and disappointment are manifestly evident in the first two essays published here. His optimistic early essay "Doing Your Will" predates his disillusionment.

Jack Parsons' death was quickly ruled accidental by the police; if so, it was one of the most convenient and well timed accidents in history. Despite a later press account of evidence at the scene suggesting foul play, and the suspicions of an explosives expert who knew Parsons' cautious work habits, the police declined to reopen the investigation.[6]

Parsons' genius had provided the key to the world's first reliable solid fuel rocket, developed with a bare minimum of institutional support. Parsons had only recently been caught by the FBI preparing a proposal for an Israeli rocket production facility—to which he had attached several of his own classified papers—prompting the Department of Justice to consider prosecuting him for espionage. Considering what Parsons had accomplished for America, there may have been real concern in some quarters about what he could do for the fledgling state of Israel. Surely it is not mere conspiracy theorizing to allow for the possibility that he was murdered, as his widow Cameron firmly believed.[7]

His rocketry colleague Frank Malina—the first director of JPL—left America for France to become a sculptor and UNESCO official after investigations of his youthful affiliation with the Communist party; his American passport was revoked and he was indicted in absentia by the House Un-American Activities Committee. At a 1968 event commemorating the founding of JPL, Malina remarked that "Jack

---

6. The progression is reflected in the news coverage in *The Los Angeles Times*. The issue for June 18, 1952, p. 1, has the headline "Rocket Scientist Killed in Pasadena Explosion"; June 19, p. 1, has "Scientist's Fatal Blast Explained"; June 21, p. 2, has "Mystery Angle Enters Scientist's Death Blast," adding that "Probers Advance Belief 'Someone Else' Handled Waste in Parsons' Laboratory."

7. Ibid.

Parsons made key contributions to development of propel-
lants and engines, many of which still play an important part
in space technology today. He has not yet received his due for
this pioneering work."[8] Malina partly remedied this by
arranging to have the lunar crater Parsons named in his honor
by the International Astronomical Union in 1972.

Parsons represented what was best in America. He was
childishly, exuberantly self-confident, and what he lacked in
formal education he more than made up for with his quick
mind and originality of thought. He had an undying idealistic
faith in the essential decency of his fellow men and women—he
genuinely loved his own species; not all philosophers do. He
knew that he was here on earth for a purpose, which was to
help wake everyone up to the fact that *they were too*. His rejec-
tion of the bourgeois values of security, normalcy, safe-
ty—even his own sanity, which he risked many times and
arguably lost at least once—was rooted in the terrible urgen-
cy he felt.

As a rocket scientist he had, like Vulcan, tapped into a well-
spring of power that he instinctively knew had the potential to
destroy us all. Like Prometheus, he had brought fire to earth,
with its potential to burn us down or take us to the stars. He
realized, however imperfectly, that our old value systems and
power structures were woefully inadequate to safeguard this
power and save us from ourselves. He understood that nothing short of a worldwide revolution in society as he then knew
it—repressive, conformist and stultifying to the new men and
women like himself, who represented humanity's best hope
for our future—had to take place. The modern threat of
militant religious sectarianism armed with weapons of mass
destruction is the inexorable conclusion of a trend he foresaw.

He knew from history that religion held the best potential
to achieve this change on a global scale, and took up experi-
mental theology—which is to say magick or scientific illumi-

---

8. "Story of JPL 'Birth' Told at Dedication," *The Independent* (Pasadena),
   November 1, 1968, p. 1.

nism—with the same reckless self-confidence that had served him so well as a rocket scientist. Parsons' approach was very un-Californian: he adopted an existing religion, rather than invent a new one. The religion he chose was Thelema—the new dispensation given to the world by Aleister Crowley through *The Book of the Law* in 1904, whose third and final chapter, if understood as prophetically descriptive and not prescriptive, gave a foretaste of the new world to come, one unthinkable in the early years of the 20th century but all too familiar to us today from that century's brutal history.

Parsons knew that fear would become the ultimate weapon; it would cause people to trade their dreams, their principles, their inner identities and their own purposes in life to protect themselves and their families. He had witnessed the blinding overnight successes achieved by the government-by-terror totalitarianism of Stalinist Russia and Nazi Germany. He had the foresight to see that America, once armed with the new powers of total destruction and surveillance that were sure to follow the swelling flood of new technologies, had the potential to become even more repressive unless its founding principles of individual liberty were religiously preserved and its leaders held accountable to them.

Two of the keys to redressing the balance were the freedom of women and an end to the state control of individual sexual expression. He knew that these potent forces, embodied as they are in a majority of the world's population, had the power, once unleashed, to change the world—as indeed they have in the West during the more than half-century since these essays were written. The top-down controls of the patriarchal power elites that had long suppressed them were—and still are, to varying degrees—deeply rooted in the old religions of Judaism, Christianity and Islam, whose ancient enmities still threaten the future of humanity. Hence the need for a new, universalist religion independent of gender, race or clime.

Parsons found that universal religion in Thelema. He joined the O.T.O. in 1941, and was later made acting Master of the only Lodge of the Order in the world, Agape Lodge, which he had helped relocate to an impressive mansion with extensive grounds in Pasadena. As an O.T.O. initiate Parsons was sworn to defend the Rights of Man, which Crowley had first enshrined in O.T.O.'s secret initiations around 1918–19.

Crowley firmly believed in talismanic publications and their power to change the world. To counter totalitarianism during World War II he made the Rights of Man public, in a pamphlet issued jointly by the O.T.O. in London and California entitled *Liber Oz*, also known as *The Book of the Goat*—an animal noted for its independence and self-reliance, *Oz* being the Hebrew for goat. Its publication in 1941—the year Parsons joined the O.T.O.—is significant, as Parsons was caught up in the current of heady excitement that its publication generated.

Writing to Gerald J. Yorke, Crowley described *Liber Oz* as the "O.T.O. plan in words of one syllable," with five sections: moral freedom, bodily freedom, mental freedom and sexual freedom, ending with what he called the "safeguard tyrannicide": "Man has the right to kill those who would thwart these rights"—i.e., totalitarian tyrants. Yorke objected that it would be "almost impossible to do anything without clashing with somebody." Crowley replied, "Of course, [...] but this is because the rule is not accepted. Same applies to cricket, or machines. Our claim is that the system minimizes friction."[9]

If some rights enumerated in *Liber Oz* such as "Man has the right to draw as he will" seem trivial, consider history: Jack Parsons' widow, the artist Cameron (1922–1995), exhibited a drawing that caused the Los Angeles Police vice squad to raid the Ferus Gallery in 1957 on grounds of obscenity. She was vindicated in a landmark First Amendment free-speech court precedent.

Crowley considered the provision for human rights in the United Nations charter of 1945—enshrining "universal respect for, and observance of, human rights and fundamental freedoms for all without distinction as to race, sex, language, or religion"—to be magical fruit of the seed planted

---

9. Crowley to Gerald J. Yorke, September 13, 1941.

by *Liber Oz*. But he believed that it fell short of embracing the full Rights of Man. He died in December 1947, and a year later the United Nations adopted its Universal Declaration of Human Rights—a major advance towards Crowley's ideal, but with misplaced emphasis: in it, the states grant rights to their citizens, rather than citizens entrusting the state with management of their inalienable rights. Human rights were also made subject to "the just requirements of morality, public order and the general welfare in a democratic society"—a provision since used to justify atrocities like the Tienanmen Square massacre.

Parsons' best-known essay, "Freedom is a Two-Edged Sword,"[10] is published here with "Freedom is a Lonely Star"; they should be read together, as each complements the other in important ways. "Sword" is, in part, a commentary on *Liber Oz*, which is paraphrased closely on pp. 25–26.

Parsons was a charismatic orator, and gave memorable lectures to the members of Agapé Lodge, where he produced his earliest writings. An example of his early political thought, written when he was only thirty, is a lecture delivered on July 31, 1945, retitled "Doing Your Will" for inclusion in this volume.[11] He truly shone as a conversationalist, his mind soaring late into the night as he talked with friends and fellow members in the parlor and around the dining table, much as he is doing in the frontispiece photograph to this edition.

Parsons' impassioned pleas for a sane world still resonate with power, as the dangers he foresaw have not yet passed.

Hymenaeus Beta
Frater Superior, O.T.O.

---

10. John Whiteside Parsons, *Freedom is a Two-Edged Sword and Other Essays (The Oriflamme* 1), ed. Cameron and Hymenaeus Beta (Las Vegas and New York: New Falcon Publications in association with Ordo Templi Orientis, 1989; rpt. 2001).

11. Titled "Lecture III" in typescript, it was the fourth of a weekly series of ten lectures, of which six survive. It was first published as "The Agapé Lectures (Excerpt)" in *The Magical Link* VIII(4) (1994–95), pp. 1–2. The first three paragraphs are omitted as they discuss the previous lecture; section numbers have been added for clarity.

FREEDOM IS A
LONELY STAR

Freedom is a Lonely Star

ONE TIME, IN AMERICA, there was a dream. It was a dream of man. Through the long night, through two thousand years of bondage, the dream was born. Out of agony and terror. Out of poverty and misery. Out of secret thoughts, in the heart of despair. Out of whispered words, in the shadow of death. Out of love, in an empire of hate. Children, chained to work carts. Women whipped through the streets. Men and women, and children too, burned alive in the public square, because they dared to think of freedom.

Lonely, and difficult, and dangerous, through ages and ages of night the star of freedom was born. Nursed with blood. Nourished on agony. Carried, at length, to a new world, and planted there, in the fresh soil. Nourished, until it shone with an awesome light, a winged thing so high, so pure, so beautiful that it struck all the world with wonder. A dream of free men, working together in dignity and significance of honorable representatives, who cherished freedom and honor beyond their own interest and welfare. Of the inviolability of individual freedom, beyond kings and priests, beyond politicians and judges, beyond money or power or prestige. And all over the world men in tyranny and ignorance and oppression responded to that dream. "At last," they said, "at last."

Fragments of the dream come down to us now — "We hold that all men are born free and equal; and endowed...with certain inalienable rights, among which are the right to life, *liberty* and the pursuit of happiness."[12] "I shall guard even my enemy from oppression."[13] "Give me liberty or give me death."[14] Fragments and strands, echoing emptily in empty hearts.

---

12. [Parsons' paraphrase of the Declaration of Independence; emphasis his.]

13. [Paraphrase of Thomas Paine, "He that would make his own liberty secure must guard even his enemy from oppression; for if he violates this duty he establishes a precedent that will reach to himself."]

14. [Patrick Henry, in a 1775 speech.]

For the dream is dead now, or in a sleep that is like unto death. It has been sold out, denied and betrayed.

It has been sold out by cheap and venal politicians, by benevolent authoritarians, by "loyal" party men, by shrewd and greedy capitalists, by wise guys and smart guys that know all the answers. It has been sold out by the great middle class that prefers its false security and false freedom, by the labor leaders that put power first, and the little man who prefers—at last with at least a decent reason—a full belly, or the promise of a fully belly, to freedom turned dangerous and hungry.

It has been sold out by America, and for that reason the heart of America is sick and the soul of America is dead. It is for this reason that we cannot instruct our children with a significant morality, or elect honorable men to office, or conduct our own affairs with a sense of dignity and significance. That dream itself was the soul of America, in which there was no cause but man, no religion but man, and no goal but man. The betrayal of his dream is the one thing that man cannot forgive himself. The pompous oratory, the brave show, the frantic search for scapegoats and traitors—all attempts to conceal from himself the thing that cannot be concealed, his cowardice, his failure.

Having failed freedom at home, we engaged in sick and fevered attempts to impose it abroad, with all the panoply of futility. Out of the First World War, national prohibition, the income tax, Mussolini, Franco, Hitler, and the benevolent dictatorship of the New Deal. Out of the Second, Stalin, the enslavement of sciences, and the suppression of all freedoms in the Great Red Scare. After the Third, what will be left to suppress? Heroic Crusades for Freedom. Advances to the rear. For what? Survival? To what end? To the end that we must ape the enemy in order to defeat him on the grounds that *our* ends justify our means? To the very end, where all our freedoms are gone, the betrayers themselves betrayed, and freedom again rediscovered and reconsecrated in agony and blood? To what their end?

Perhaps we could face the world as conquerors, in the name of power and right, if we had the guts, which we do not. We could face the world as heroes if we had the courage of our own dream; which we do not. But as champions of freedom abroad who have sold out freedom at home, willing to sell out the freedom of anyone else where our own ends are served, we make a sorry show. Pretentious hypocrites, lacking even the shrewdness of a sound ego, we make ourselves ridiculous in the eyes of the world. And underneath the pretense: shame — the shame of the booby that has sold out, that has bought a gold brick, that has sold his freedom, his dignity, his individuality for conformity, for money, for the prestige of the pigsty.

The principles of freedom are forever the same, but its issues are constantly shifting. George III is not the tyrant today, nor Madison the arch-reactionary, nor are we asked to surrender our liberties and persecute those who think differently because of the menace of Danton, Maurat and Robespierre. It is now safe to enshrine those persons whom once it would have been very dangerous to know — neither Washington, nor Jefferson, nor Henry nor Paine would have been "safe" or "secure" associations in the days of the revolutions.

Now there is a theory that our fathers fought and died for our freedom, and thus bought it for us. So now there is no need for us to concern ourselves with that for which they paid with discomfort, hunger and blood. We can leave this to those who are hired or drafted to protect our liberty.

We are assured on every hand that we are a free people — in fact, we have it in writing. Our fathers were not content with such assurances, but rather, by act and deed, assured these freedoms for themselves. That is the difference.

We are a savage culture. Our emotions and our attitudes, our needs and our drives, are all savage. Our religions and our morals, societies and creeds, cults and taboos: all are those of the savage.

But we are savages who have assumed the pretense of civilization, and this is our great disaster. This miserable pretense has closed at once both possibilities of stabilizing our culture. The one, or the non-pretentious savage outlet, would allow us the expression of our savage needs and drives in a set of acceptable mores and expectations. The other, an acceptance of our savagery together with an aspiration to true civilization, might allow us to face and know ourselves, and in the slow, painful laboratory where all natural processes are wrought, in time effect some upward change.

But in our blindness to our savagery we are trapped — we refuse to see the facts until it is too late — until in our private lives the impossible attention undoes our fairest hopes and fondest dreams, and in the public scene the idiot and criminal nations play holocaust with all our world. And now, as by a joke of the gods, a power that is sublime has been put in the hands of our most ruthless criminals and our most appalling idiots. It thus becomes clear that we must soon choose openly the most abysmal savagery without the least vestige of further pretense, or we must renounce savagery to an undreamed of degree. And in this renunciation we must accept two propositions of true civilizations: the inviolability of the individual, and the absolute necessity for a world state.

No conceivable conquest, save the conquest of the individual of and by himself, can assure us against destruction in the conflicts to come. And if this conquest cannot be total, it must be sufficient to produce the requisite number of adequate and civilized individuals.

At present, I cannot conceive of a workable world state, and I know that it cannot be conceived and ordered in a world of savages. But I can conceive that individuals, sufficiently evolved, and working towards the understanding, knowledge, and self control that defines freedom, could achieve this. It can only be done by free men, and these men must be equally free of the pretense and self-deception, and the success and conformity cults that have made our society culture a slough of despond. The inane and illogical restrictions that repress all individuality and creative spirit, the savage cruelty and hostility to ourselves and our fellows, the terror and guilt that ride us like nightmares, must be understood and relieved.

That such an undertaking would be popular is hardly to believed. That it would succeed in one generation, or ten, is perhaps too much to expect. But it is the only way. The wars, revolutions, crimes, the social and economic disorders and inequalities, which the ignorant regard as causes in themselves, are only the manifestations of the savage fact behind the civilized pretense — outbursts made more furious by evasions and repression. I know of no other answer than to cry a last crusade, a crusade for freedom, for the freedom to know and be ourselves before it is forever too late. If there is a hope, that hope is in man, and it is only in free men that the hope can be realized.

It is my aim to offer an examination of pretenses whereby they can no longer be concealed by institutions and names, and a definition of freedom that will, once and for all, place it beyond equivocation and deceit.

The conditioned reflex response of the standard ego is formulated in terms of the cross, the flag, the home, the church, the school, God, mothers and American womanhood. These things have a purely reflex value, without any rationale whatsoever. No standard ego has ever examined them; it would be heretical to do so. He simply responds. Behind these mechanical values, the necessities of life are met with rationalization processes that are often almost sublime. The crooked business and political deals, murder and pillage, seductions, rapes and visits to prostitutes are all conducted by the man who isn't there, in another world whose doors are guarded by the most marvelous network of hypocrisy, pretense and downright lying ever invented by the mind of man.

Occasionally some venturesome soul, dissatisfied with the standard ego formulations, breaks out and wanders around in reality awhile, until he is frightened back into the dream again or guided back by some psychiatrist.

The first view of truth is terror — that knowledge is as old as time — all the myths show it. From alcoholism to paranoid psychosis, from the mildest neurotic syndrome to schizophrenia, the escape is from the terror of the true self and the true world. Dalua and Dermot, Pan and Persephone, Mayan and Mixitli, Janicot and Jehovah, each showed a visage of horror before the true face—the total truth—was revealed. Truth, in short, is not for fools and cowards, but for this the will that acts, the wisdom that knows, and the courage that dares the first terrible impact.

Beyond the fanged serpent are the immortal meadows, behind the skull face lie the stars. Only the free man shall pass that portal, and walk out into the total world that is eternity.

In a world where a precocious romance is set above reality—where He is a God and She is a Goddess in a springtime, where all endings are happy, plain John Smith and Mary Jones have short shrift. Mortality cannot endure the comparison—a clumsy overture, a cold in the nose, an unexpected monthly ruins the enchantment, and the movies assure us that our mate, odious comparison, is somehow a miserable exception to the golden rule.

But whether we seek the dream in an escape from reality, or whether we cynically deny it, we are equally damned. True marriage, that rare estate, is as close to paradise as humanity can come. But it cannot be attained by the pretense of romance or the pretense of cynicism. It can be attained only by keeping the vision of beauty constantly before us and by transmitting, by constant effort and courage, by faith and love, the hard matters of reality into the shape of the beloved dream. And that marriage attained is the garden of paradise, whereof happy children are the "fruit."

It is not easily come to—it is possible only to courage, to maturity, to intelligence and high idealism. But it can be attained, "and if it can it must," for that marriage is the sure foundation of a free world.

Police, like the military, are a necessary evil that requires constant surveillance and rigid control in order to keep them within the bounds of constitutional law and democratic procedure. In most large American cities, police are little more than the agents of a corrupt political machine, acting as collectors and supervisors for organized prostitution, gambling, dope and protection rackets. For these gangsters, the collection of revenue and the terrorization of opposition is of far greater importance than the suppression of crime. The police mind is usually of a sadistic and homicidal trend, and the office, as it now exists, offers an ideal opportunity for the expressions of the urge, and the ruthless punishment of symbolic scapegoats in the form of prostitutes, derelicts, Negroes, radicals, drunks, and other helpless and insignificant members of the nation indivisible, with liberty and justice for all.

The traditional American distrust and dislike of police stems from a remembrance of the police states of Europe. But the modern American has abrogated, along with his other freedoms, his freedom from police interference in his private life, unwarranted search and seizure, wiretapping, suspension of constitutional immunity (the sole guarantee against intimidation and torture), and all the other trappings of a police state. His present resentment is about as mature, as courageous, and as effective as that of a small, broken-spirited boy against a brutal and tyrannical father. This gutless specimen is now engaged in selling out each liberty that someone else gained for him, as fast he can make the deal. He is buying security, protection, prosperity — the fine futile freedoms — and all the other gangsters goods at a bargain price. All that he pays is his right to call himself a man.

The methods by which politicians achieve their ultimate ambitions, that is, to become tyrants, are obvious, and exceedingly stale. But however old the trick, it seems that there is always a fresh crop of suckers. Foremost among the public plans and promises of Mussolini, Hitler and Stalin on their way to power were *not* the establishment of concentration camps, the murder and torture of free citizens, and the annihilation of all freedom.

As hard as it may seem to believe, by some sort of anachronistic plagiarisms these plans and promises included increased prosperity, fewer slums, social security, more jobs, and defense against enemies without and traitors within.

These were also among the foremost plans and promises of Sulla, Caesar, Robespierre and Napoleon. The bait is so old and so obvious one suspects that repetition must have given it prestige. The first step is the discovery of an emergency. Any emergency will do—a depression, a plot, an enemy without, an enemy within, the second coming of Christ, witches—anything whatever which can be used to whip fear, hatred and hysteria to fever pitch.

The next step is the program to meet the emergency. Whatever the program may be, increased taxation is its inevitable first-born and best beloved. Taxation—that is, for the Great Cause—taxation to create bureaus which create bureaus that require taxation for the support of bureaus. Taxation for the support of more politicians, police, tax collectors, investigators, employment aids, pensions, charities, public works, et cetera. Taxation, in short, for anything and everything. Purely, of course, as a temporary measure. Ah, these temporary measures. How permanent they are. The Republicans procedures of Rome were suspended, just temporarily, so that the politicians could fight a war and save the country in "this great and terrible emergency." But somehow the emergency lasted through Sulla and Caesar, and Augustus, and Tiberius, and Caligula, and Claudius and Nero and in fact, clean through the collapse and final dissolution of the Roman state.

The next step is the discovery that the emergency is much worse than anyone thought. Revolution is on the verge, collapse is imminent, the world is going to end tomorrow. So naturally we will *act now* and in order to do this it is necessary to have a dictatorship. Harsh word? Shall we say—organizations to meet the emergency temporarily, of course. The sophistries by which this putsch is justified, palliated, honey coated, are among the most ludicrous in the politician's bag of tricks.

The church, for example, burnt heretics from motives of most terrible mercy. Since this was the only way to save their souls from hell, of course the church didn't really kill, she only tried, convicted and sentenced to execution. The state did the dirty work, just to keep the church's hands clean. Execution was by fire, because the church could not of course condone the shedding of blood.

The dictatorship of the proletariat is merely temporary—the state will gradually wither away like a snark hunter, leaving us all as free as birds. Meanwhile it may be necessary to kill, torture and imprison a few million people, but whose fault is it if they get in the way of progress? Socialism—the greatest good of the greatest number—how can you argue against it? That only proves that you are in the minority, in the wrong.

When the rights of labor interfere with the public good, the national need, the emergency—then to hell with their rights. What does the freedom of a few radical university professors, scientists, teachers, government workers matter when our country is in danger? Sign or be fired. And whose freedom tomorrow, fatheads, fools? Whose rights when the masks are down and the gloves off, and a spade is the thing you dig your grave with? When a man can be fired, hounded, persecuted, jailed in America for the opinions he holds, for his refusal to have his privacy violated, then it is time to publicly burn the Bill of Rights and the Declaration of Independence, and call this country by its right name—a tyrant state.

How can we cope with these predators, politicians and their moronic dupes? We can examine their emergencies, for what they are worth. Predators are not confined to one party or one nation. There is always the real need to be well armed, well informed and well prepared against *all* enemies of freedom. Well meaning fools, appalled by the predators within, clamor to throw down their arms and welcome the predators without. This is plain suicide, but the fear of predators without can also drive fools to the same suicide within. Arms and armies are necessary, but it is also necessary to watch them, to control them, and to keep them subservient to the private citizens whom they serve.

We can reduce political sophistries to their basic elements, and examine them in the light of reason and necessity.

Politicians need some graft—some excitement, some opportunity for hysteria; it is their life blood. A certain degree of criminality and psychosis goes with the breed. But easily, easily, gentlemen. Within limits, and under control.

Taxation, however, is a major root of the politician's power, and it is here that he can best be regulated. The first new limit on potential power must be the abolition of confiscatory taxation, and of punitive taxation in all forms. Taxation should exist for the sole purpose of raising reasonable revenue, and must in no case exceed a fixed and minimum percentage of income, profit, value, or sales. The moment it does, it becomes a weapon of dictatorship, superseding and replacing due process of law.

Taxation must be open, not hidden and secret. The process of withholding taxes from wages is a violation of individual and corporate rights, a dodge to dupe employees into blaming employers for the piratical raids of government on income. The income tax itself was the opening wedge in a conspiracy to build a vast politico-economic empire, wielding an absolute control over the income, business and private life of every citizen. Augmented by social security and old age and a multitude of hidden taxes, its success is now reasonably apparent to all except the chronic paupers and welfare dupes that are its dubious beneficiaries. It's such fun to soak the rich. But not so much fun when a rich man, from a tax standpoint, is anyone with an income over fifty dollars a month. Let the common man pay his taxes in the open, and he will soon see that his "security," at that price, could be sold by any insurance company, engraved on tablets of pure gold, at a handsome profit.

Any successful confidence game must be played in stages; the sucker is not hooked all at once. The first issue must be one in which we all believe, the first victim someone we all hate. A rich man, a radical, an atheist, a Negro, a Jew—some no good bastard. *We* are all together, on the other side, until we take the bait. Then *we* are on the hook, and it is too late. The Nazi party was the government, the government makes the law, and good citizens always obey the law. Q.E.D.

concentration camps = good government. That is the lesson of history, fresh, this time from Germany. One day it may be very well said of us also, "it is too bad they could not learn." On the basis of the present trend, I would give this country fifteen years, at the outside, to turn into something that that is in essence a socialist or a fascist state.

History is curious. A few of the right men might stop it—the old dream still burns in America, if deep down and dimly. But they have not yet appeared.

The advent of psychoanalytical sciences and the publication of the Kinsey Report have indicated a true state of culture morals previously unsuspected in western history. The impact of these events on society is of a moment comparable to that of nuclear physics and the advent of the atomic bomb. The significance of these revolutionary findings in the field of morals has not yet reached the point of practical application in terms of large scale individual and social adjustment. Confusion in regard to proper and significant attitudes and behavior appears to have reached an all-time high.

In addition to the tremendous burdens of self control imposed by culture and civilization, man now sees himself restricted by moral concepts which now appear savage, pretentious and archaic. In the face of ever-increasing social complexity, this burden becomes intolerable and he is tempted to throw the whole thing over at the first clean opportunity. This danger is particularly great because of lack of discrimination between what is essential and what is superfluous in the field of morals. The need for cooperation and renunciation exists as never before; as a corollary, the need for freedom and individuality, wherever these are possible, is of the same magnitude. It is in the field of sexual morals that unnecessary restrictions are most severe, and it is in this field that a process of revision and liberation can go the furthest, and serve the most immediate purpose.

It would be of little value, and perhaps almost a disservice, to further demonstrate the barbarous nature and the failure of western sex morals, to develop a further philosophy of sexual freedom and stay at that. This would only serve to increase the awareness of frustration and unhappiness, without indicating any way out of the morass. In addition, it is necessary to clearly show a practical, individual solution to the moral problem, and that is the object of our work.

And you, man, put off this longing for your mother, put away these childish things and come up into your manhood. She is not won by small devices and petty conceits, nor by crying, nor by beating on the chest, nor by roses or by gold, but by the clean, bright steel of the sword of freedom. Freedom of yourself, in yourself.

If you have manhood she will look to you for guidance, if you have courage she will find security with you, and if you have freedom she will come with you to liberty in all the spheres. On these three points will you win and hold her and not otherwise, the woman whom your manhood desires.

And from this marriage and not otherwise will come the children who will make a new world, the redeemers of prophecy, the conquerors of darkness and fear.

And thus and not otherwise, in freedom, in love, in brotherhood and in the marriage of true minds, will we come finally, unobstructed, to the stars.

FREEDOM IS A
TWO-EDGED SWORD

Preface

SINCE I FIRST WROTE THIS ESSAY IN 1946, some of my most ominous predictions have been all too grimly fulfilled. Public employees have been subjected to the ignominy and indignity of "loyalty" oaths and "loyalty purges." Members of the United States Senate, moving under the cloak of "immunity" and the excuse of "emergency," have made a joke of justice and a mockery of privacy. Constitutional immunity and legal procedure have been consistently violated, and that which once, not so long ago, would have been a universal outrage in America, is today refused even a review by the Supreme Court.

The golden voice of social security —of socialized this and socialized that, with its attendant confiscatory taxation and intrusion on individual liberty—is everywhere raised and everywhere heeded. England has entered the aegis of a regime synonymous with total regimentation. Austria, Hungary, Yugoslavia and Czechoslovakia have fallen victims to Communism, and the United States is in the process of making deals with the barbarous and corrupt dictatorships of Argentina and Spain.

As I write, the United States Senate is pursuing a burlesque investigation into the sphere of private sexual morals, which, for all its buffoonery, will cause pain and sorrow to many innocent persons, in an intolerable and grotesque invasion of their rights.

The inertia and acquiescence which allows the almost complete suspension of our liberties would once have been unthinkable. The present ignorance and indifference is appalling and almost unbelievable. That little which is worthwhile in civilization and culture is made possible by the few who are capable of creative thinking and independent action, with the grudging assistance of the rest. When the majority

17

of men surrender their freedom, barbarism is near; when the minority surrender it, we are in the dark ages. Even the word liberalism is suspect through the unmitigated effort of fuzzy heads who believe it synonymous with Russian boot-licking, and humanism is no more than a front for the totalism of the church.

Science, that was going to save the world back in H.G. Wells' time, is regimented, strait-jacketed, scared shitless, its universal language diminished to one word: security.

In this 1950 view, some of my more hopeful utterances may appear almost naïve. However, I was never so naïve as to believe that freedom, in any full sense of the word, is possible to more than a few. But I have believed and do believe that these few — by self-sacrifice, by wisdom, by courage, by continuous and tremendous effort — can achieve and maintain a free world. The labor is heroic, but it can be done; by example and by education, it can be achieved. This is the faith that built America; this is the faith that America has surrendered; and this is the faith that I call on America to renew or perish.

We are one nation, and one world. The soul of the slums looks out of the eyes of Wall Street, and the fate of a Chinese coolie determines the destiny of America. We cannot suppress our brothers' liberty without murdering ourselves. We will stand together, as men, for human freedom and human dignity, or we will fall together, simians all, back to the swamp.

In this late, this very late hour, it is with solutions that we must be primarily concerned. I seem to be living in a nation that simply does not know what freedom is.

We believe that it is a word, a piece of paper, something we are told that we have, that we tell each other we have. Indeed, it is more — far more — than that.

It is to that object — to the definition of freedom, to its understanding, in order that it may be attained and defended — that this essay is devoted. I need not add that freedom is a dangerous thing. But it is hardly possible that we are all cowards.

I
A Sword Is Drawn

For numberless centuries society unquestioningly accepted the proposition that certain men were created to be slaves, whose natural function was to serve priests and kings, nobles and great lords, men of substance and property that were appointed slavemasters by almighty God. Further, this system was reinforced by the established doctrines that all men and women were owned, their minds by the church, their bodies by the state. This convenient situation was supported by a considerable body of authority, morals, religion and philosophy.

Against this doctrine, some two hundred years ago, was openly raised the most astonishing heresy the world has ever known: the principle of liberalism. In essence, this principle stated that all men were created equal, and endowed with inalienable rights. The words inalienable rights mean rights which cannot be taken away, which belong to a man, as his birthright.

This principle appealed to certain intractable spirits—heretics, atheists and revolutionaries—and has since, in spite of the opposition of the majority of organized society, made some headway. As a doctrine, it has become so popular that it is rendered lip service by all the major states.

But it is still so distasteful to persons in authority and seeking authority that it is nowhere embodied as a fundamental law, and is continuously violated in letter and in spirit by every trick and expedient of bigotry and reaction. Further, absolutist and totalitarian groups of the most vicious nature use liberalism as a cloak under which they move to re-establish tyrannies and extinguish the liberty of all opponents.

Thus, religious groups seek to abrogate freedom of art, speech and the press, reactionaries move to suppress labor, and communists to establish dictatorships—all in the name of freedom. Thus, because of the peculiar distinctions given to freedom by some of these camouflaged tyrants, it seems

necessary to redefine freedom in terms in which it was understood by that depraved cynic Voltaire, the dirty atheist Paine,
the traitor Washington, the radical revolutionary Jefferson
and the anarchist Emerson.

Freedom is a two-edged sword of which one edge is liberty and the other responsibility, on which both edges are
exceedingly sharp, and which is not easily handled by casual,
cowardly or treacherous hands. For it has been sharpened by
many conflicts, tempered in many fires, quenched by much
blood, and although it is always ready for the use of the courageous and high-hearted, it will not remain when the spirit
that forged it is gone.

Now since all tyrannies are based on dogmas—that is, on
fundamental statements of absolute fact—and since all dogmas are based on lies, it behooves us first to seek for truth,
and freedom will not be far away. And the truth is that we
know nothing.

Objectively, we know nothing at all. Any system of intellectual thought—whether it be science, logic, religion, or
philosophy—is based on certain fundamental ideas or axioms which are assumed, but which cannot be proved. This is
the grave of all positivism.

We assume, but we do not *know*, that there is a real and
objective world outside our own mind. Ultimately, we do not
know what we are, or what the world is. Further, if there is
a real world apart from ourselves, we cannot know what that
is; all we know is what we perceive it to be.

All that we perceive is conveyed by our senses and interpreted by our brain. And however fine, exact or delicate our
instruments may be, they are still perceived by these senses
and interpreted by that brain. However useful, spectacular or
necessary our ideas and experiments may be, they still have
nothing to do with absolute truth or authority. Such a thing
can only exist for the individual, according to his whim or
fancy, or his inner perception of his own truth in being.

The witches and devils of the middle ages were real by
our own standards; all reputable and respectable persons
believed in them. They were seen, their effects observed, and

they perfectly accounted for a large body of otherwise inexplicable phenomena. Their existence was accepted without question by the majority of men, great and humble, and from this majority there was not, and still is not, any appeal.

Yet we do not believe in these things today. We believe in other things, similarly explaining the same phenomena. Tomorrow we will believe in still other things. We believe, but we do not know.

All our deductions—for example the theories of gravitation—are based on observed statistics, on tendencies observed to occur in a certain way. But even if our observations are correct, we do not know why these things happen, or if they have always done so, or that they will continue to do so. All our theories are only assumptions, however reasonable they may seem.

There is a sort of truth, based on experience: we know that we feel hot, or hungry, or in love. But these feelings cannot by any means be conveyed to anyone who has not experienced them. We can describe them in terms of other things familiar to him; we can analyze their cause-and-effect according to mutually acceptable theories. But he will not have the vaguest idea of what the feeling is like.

These may be very negative considerations, but within their limits we can deduce very positive principles.

1. Whatever the universe is, we are either all or part of it, by virtue of our consciousness. But we do not know which.

2. No philosophy, theory, religion or system of thought can be absolute and infallible. They are relative only. One man's opinion is just as good as another's.

3. There is no absolute justification for emphasizing one individual theory or way of life over another.

4. Every man has the right to his own opinion and his own way of life. There is no system of human thought which can successfully refute this thesis.

That much for positivism. But other things remain. There are necessity, expediency and convenience. If these are illusions, they are still very popular illusions, and it is usual to consider them. Politics is concerned with necessity and expediency, whereas science is concerned with convenience.

This is not, however, intended to discredit science and reason in their proper spheres. Reason is one of our greatest gifts — the power that differentiates us from the animals. And science is our greatest tool, and our best hope for building a genuine civilization. (It is curious that this modern truism appears, in this system of reasoning, as a concession.)

But in spite of its inestimable value, science is a tool, and has nothing to do with ultimate truth. Herein is the danger of science. As a tool it is so valuable, so useful and so irresistible that we incline to regard it as the arbiter of the absolute, giving final and irrefutable pronouncement on all things. This is exactly the position that the pedant, the dogmatist and the dialectical materialist would have us take. Then, posing as a "scientist" or propounding "scientific" doctrine, he can persuade us to accept his values and obey his orders. Today must forever be free to overthrow its yesterdays. Otherwise it will degenerate into ancestor worship.

But it is necessary that we defend freedom, unless we all wish to be slaves. It is expedient that we achieve brotherhood, unless we desire destruction. And it is convenient that we grant others the right to their own opinions and lives, in order to maintain our own.

The intelligent individual will not base his conduct on an arbitrary or absolute concept of right and wrong. It may be argued that all motives and all actions are selfish, since they are intended to satisfy some requirement of the ego. Perhaps this is true of self-sacrifice, abnegation and the highest altruism. We engage in these things in order to satisfy ourselves, to attain some object.

The ego may be very broad. A man may include the whole world as a part of his ego, and set out to redeem or save this world for no other reason than that he gain pleasure from this idea. Such a man, far from being unselfish, is extremely egotistical. Even the artist, devoted to the production of pure beauty, is so because of his need and his nature. At least such egotism is not petty.

The motives of family, love and patriotism are all rooted in biology. This does not necessarily detract from such actions and motives. Everything in nature is beautiful, and it is no less beautiful because it is understood.

But the stupid man will assign arbitrary values to all things, in order to protect and justify his own position. His morals are based on things which he wishes were true, or which someone else wishes were true. His philosophy pays no attention to relative facts or realities. But in his life he must deal with relative facts and realities, and consequently he is constantly involved with pretenses and evasions.

The enlightened liberal needs no such justification. He will realize and accept his inherent selfishness, and the inherent selfishness of all men. He will understand living as technique—the technique of getting what he wants on the terms he wants.

Stealing may be the most direct means of acquiring property, but unless he steals a considerable amount, a prison sentence is a possible corollary of his action. On the other hand, he may observe with dismay the subtle disintegration of character attendant upon the so-called legitimate business life.

His problem, then, is not only to acquire the things he needs, but to get them in some entertaining or at least non-devastating manner. Perhaps he will decide it is not worth the effort. But in all problems, there is no question of right involved. There is only the question of technique, and of cost.

Such is the case with freedom. If we abrogate another's freedom to gain our ends, our own freedom is thereby jeopardized. That is the cost. If we wish to secure our own freedom, we must assure all men's freedom. That is the technique.

If a liberal were to develop two personalities, and one of those personalities established a benevolent dictatorship while the other continued his liberal activities, it would be only a matter of time until he killed himself.

The restriction of others' freedom is self-enslavement and suicide. The dictator is the most abject of slaves.

These simple considerations are the logical basis of the philosophy of liberalism.

From such considerations, and from many more, the fundamental principles of liberalism arise as a code of rights basic in nature and clear beyond misconception.

This code must be the law and beyond the law, an ultimate expression of the dignity and inviolability of the individual. It must be above the meddlings of courts and lawyers, beyond the whim of the populace and the treachery of demagogues and dictators. It must be the epitome of man's aspirations toward liberty and self-determination, so sacred that its violation by a state, group, or individual is treason and sacrilege.

The Bill of Rights in the American Constitution is a step in this direction, and its study will indicate a more final development. But in a world so threatened by positivism and paternalism, this document is limited both in scope and application.

It permits such violations of liberty as the late national Prohibition Law, the Draft Law, the closed shop, the Mann Act, censorship laws, anti-firearms laws and racial discrimination.

It has been said, with justification, that the Constitution means what the Supreme Court says it means. A document so fundamental as a Bill of Rights cannot be jeopardized by arbitrary interpretations. It should need no interpretations. It must apply equally to the state, and to every state, municipality, official, group and individual within the state. It must apply in such a way that the individual or minority need not [have] recourse to elaborate, lengthy and costly proceedings in order to protect these rights.

It is the duty of the state to provide this recourse to all alike, in the same manner and to better purpose than life and property are now protected, from the more obvious and poorly organized forms of violence.

Freedom cannot be subject to arbitrary interpretation and misinterpretation. It must plainly include freedom from persecution on moral, political, economic, racial, social or religious grounds.

No man, no group, and no nation has the right to any man's individual freedom. No matter how pure the motive, how great the emergency, how high the principle, such action is nothing but tyranny. It is never justified.

The question is: are we able to face the consequences of democracy? Nor is it sufficient that freedom be assured by purely negative means. Freedom is meaningless where its expression is controlled by powerful groups such as the press, the radio, the motion pictures, churches, politicians and capitalists. Freedom must be ensured.

And it can only be ensured by allegiance to the principle that man has certain inalienable rights, among which are the rights: [15]

To live his private life, insofar as it concerns only himself, as he sees fit. To eat and drink, to dress, live and travel as, where and how he will.

To express himself, as he sees fit. To speak, write, print, experiment and otherwise create as he will.

To work as he chooses, when he chooses, and where he chooses, at a reasonable and commensurate wage.

To purchase his food, shelter, medical and social needs, and all other services and commodities necessary to his existence and self expression, at a reasonable and commensurate price.

To a decent environment and upbringing during his childhood, until he reaches a responsible majority.

To love as he sees fit, where, how and with whom he chooses, in accordance only with the desires of himself and his partner.

To the positive opportunity to enjoy these rights, as he sees fit, without obstruction on the one hand, or compulsion on the other.

---

15. [These rights are a paraphrase of those enumerated in Aleister Crowley's *Liber Oz*; see p. 68.]

To protect his person, his property and his rights, to the extent of killing the aggressor, if necessary. This is the purpose of the right to keep and bear arms.

These rights must be counterbalanced by certain responsibilities.

The liberal, accepting them, must guarantee these rights to all others at all times, regardless of his personal feelings or interests.

He must work to establish and protect them, live in a manner commensurate with them, and be prepared to defend them with his life.

He must refuse allegiance to any state or organization which denies these rights, and aid and encourage all who, without qualification or equivocation, endorse them. He must refuse to compromise these principles on any issues, or for any reason.

Such is the sword of freedom. It is two-edged; a weapon for heroes. Such principles are only possible to the highest types of a civilization, and difficult enough for them.

But nothing short of such principles will assure the survival of liberty, of democracy, or of society itself. Liberalism is not only a code for individuals and a state; it is the only possible basis for international civilization.

Such principles — [like] all principles — are barren unless they are revered and protected by those to whom they apply; unless they are informed by a mature and civilized outlook. They must be interpreted and applied with understanding and sympathy, with humor and tolerance. They do not need pretentiousness, sentimentality or hysterics in their application and defense. Insufferable bastards of high principle are sufficiently numerous as it is.

Nor can we force his rights upon a man. Man has the right to be a slave, if he so desires. If he does not defend his rights, he deserves slavery, and that is what he gets.

The person who is tyrannized by a member of his family or a friend, by public opinion or slave morality, is worthy of his condition, and his protestations are those of the hypocrite. Even the physically inferior person who is the subject of a bully has recourse to the equalizing effect of Judo, a knife or a gun. Any necessary means is justified if employed by the individual in defending his basic and inalienable rights.

In this respect the dueling code, with the qualifications of equalizing weapons and chivalrous conduct, may be the optimum solution to disputes which cannot be settled amicably. Such a system is undoubtedly less unfair and infinitely more determining than the elaborate, expensive and ridiculous antics of contending lawyers. Furthermore, the improvement in manners would more than compensate for the deaths of a few more hot-tempered individuals, who would otherwise probably perish in traffic disputes with far more disastrous consequences to those in the immediate vicinity.

This thesis is well illustrated if we consider the behavior of the cat. He will cooperate so far, and no further. This is his fundamental principle. He will not be pushed around. No doubt his teeth and claws, together with his willingness to use them, contribute to the practicability of this stand.

There is always one alternative to slavery: we can die fighting. No tyrant can gain more than a hollow victory against a people so committed, and even the individual can find here the ultimate rock of his inviolability.

Freedom, like charity, begins at home. No man is worthy to fight in the cause of freedom unless he has conquered his internal masters. He must learn control and discipline over the disastrous passions that would lead him to folly and ruin. He must conquer inordinate vanity and anger, self-deception, fear and inhibition. These are the crude ores of his being.

He must smelt these ores in the fire of life, forge his own sword, temper it, and sharpen it against the hard abrasive of experience. Only then is he fit to bear arms in the larger battle. There is no substitute for courage, and the victory is to the high-hearted.

He will have nothing to do with the asceticisms or the excesses of weakness. Self-expression will be his watchword, a self-expression tempered, keen and strong. First he must know and rule himself. Only then can he cope with the economic pressures which are employed by economic groups and capitalists, or the political pressures employed by demagogues.

He may then find himself in a difficult predicament. If he calls himself a liberal, he discovers that he is supposedly committed to the foreign policy of the Russian Government.

If he opposed Soviet policy he is welcomed to the camp of the Catholic Church and the Manufacturer's Association. If he eschews both camps, he is condemned for lack of principle.

Should he support the rights of working men, or minority and racial groups, he is a "red." If at the same time he believes in constitutional government and individual rights, he is also a fascist.

Many liberals are familiar with this situation, but few seem to have deduced the conclusion. The difficulty exists in the stupid or deliberate confusion of the rights of the individual and the responsibilities of the state.

It is a sad comment on our mentality that the social reformer subscribes to total regimentation, while the alleged individualist propagandizes for total irresponsibility.

The rights of the individual can be clearly defined. His responsibilities, and the responsibilities of the state, can be clearly defined. His rights end where the next man's begin.

It is the function of the state to ensure equal rights to all. This should be very clear, and it is amazing that the issue is so confused.

In the absence of a social devotion to the principles of liberalism, positivists have usurped its name and its phrases in order to propagandize for their various totalitarianisms.

This process has been greatly aided by the pseudo-liberalism which believes that all opinion contrary to its own must be suppressed.

As I write, allegedly liberal groups are agitating for the denial of public forums to those they call fascist. Americanism societies are striving for the suppression of communist or "red" literature and speech.

Religious groups, backed by a publicity-conscious press, are constantly campaigning for the prohibition of art and literature which, as if by divine prerogative, they term "indecent," immoral or dangerous.

It would seem that all organizations are devoted to one common purpose: the suppression of freedom. Nor is their sincerity any excuse. History is a bloody testament that sincerity can achieve atrocities which cynicism could never conceive.

Each of these groups is engaged in a frantic struggle to sell out, betray or destroy the freedom which is their finest birthright, and which alone assured their present existence.

Freedom is a two-edged sword. He who believes that the absolute rightness of his belief is an authority to suppress the rights and opinions of his fellows, cannot be a liberal. Liberalism cannot exist where it violates its own principles.

It cannot exist when the emergency-monger and Utopia salesman can obtain a suspension of rights, temporary or permanent. Liberty cannot be suppressed in order to defend liberalism.

The fundamental principles of liberalism must be most clearly established and defined. The rights of man are inviolable rights, beyond the law, beyond the courts or the state, beyond the will of the majority or of God. If this is not understood, there can be no liberty. Freedom is not granted. It is the inalienable possession of every man, woman and child. It cannot be taken away. It can only be surrendered.

If we are to achieve a democracy, the rights of individuals and the responsibilities of states must be openly defined and ardently defended. It is inconceivable that men who have fought and died in a war against totalitarianism do not know what they fought for. It is a fantastic joke when the things in which they believe turn like a nightmare into the things they fought against.

Another generation has gone down in blood and agony to make the world safe. But the evil things that make the world unsafe still go uncowed and undefeated, plotting new sacrifices of misery and blood.

Nor is the guilt entirely with warmongers, plutocrats and demagogues. If a people permit exploitation and regimentation in any name, they deserve their slavery. A tyrant does not make his tyranny possible. It is made possible by the people, and not otherwise.

This is a hard truth.

But every liberal who does not support his principles with his utmost strength, intelligence and courage, contributes, however indirectly, to the failure of liberalism. In order to give such support he must know and understand liberalism as a creed, a principle, and a living philosophy.

By its very nature, liberalism is not a cut and dried system of thought. In ways it changes, as man changes. In detail it may vary from individual to individual, as those individuals vary from one another.

But there are certain principles which are unchangeable. It is my purpose to explore the nature of these principles, and describe a sword with which the liberal can adequately defend his liberalism.

Much of our modern thought is characterized by pretenses and evasions, by appeals to ultimate authorities which are illiberal, superstitious and reactionary. Often we are not aware of these thought processes. We accept ideas, authorities, catch-phrases and conditions without troubling to think or investigate. Yet these things may conceal terrible traps. We accept them as right because they have a surface agreement with the things in which we believe. We welcome the man who is for liberalism, against communism, without troubling to inquire what else he is for or against. In our blindness, we leave ourselves open to exploitation, regimentation and war.

Tumultuous developments in science and society demand a new clarity of thought, a reexamination and a reenactment of principles. It is not sufficient that a principle is sacred because it is timeworn. It must be examined, tried and tested in the fires of our new needs.

In our law, in our social and international relations, we are guilty of a myriad of barbarisms and superstitions. These things are tolerated simply because they exist, because we have become used to them, and because it is often unpleasant to face facts.

The principle developed herein is very simple. The liberty of the individual is the foundation of civilization. No true civilization is possible without this liberty, and no state, national or international, is stable in its absence. The proper relation between this liberty on the one hand, and social responsibility on the other, is the balance which will assure a stable society. And by no other means, short of the total annihilation of individuality, can this be attained.

There is no further possible evasion of nature's immemorial ultimatum: change or perish.

Out of Versailles, a faint voice crying "Time will be."

Out of Paris today, the voice of trumpets proclaiming "Time is."

But tomorrow the voice of the whirlwind shouting, "Time has been."

Against that time, a sword.

II
The Sword and the State

The state exists for the primary purpose of protecting the rights of the individual. Where it fails to fulfill this purpose, it is no more than anarchy or tyranny. All other functions of the state are subordinate to this fundamental purpose.

In the machinery provided for the function of the state, basic frameworks must be provided to safeguard the rights

1. Of weaker men against stronger men
2. Of individuals against groups
3. Of smaller groups against larger groups
4. Of individuals and groups against the state.

The foundation of the state must be a code of rights similar to those indicated in the last chapter.

The argument of anarchy—that the abolition of the state will immediately precipitate Utopia—is ridiculous. In this case the individual has no recourse against powerful groups who would assume and exceed the prerogatives of the state.

It is a dubious freedom that allows a baby to toddle among wolves.

On the other hand, positivists argue that man achieves freedom by submitting to authority. Through blind obedience to the dictatorship of the proletariat, the Church, the Reich and the state will gradually wither away; the millennium will be established. Bind the child's feet, they argue, until he reaches his majority, then see him walk.

The reactionary would compromise these two extremes, binding his feet and then turning him loose to the wolves.

Much of this absurd thinking has been due to the confusion between the spheres of the individual and the state.

In reality, the distinctions are most clear.

Within the sphere of his private rights, as already defined, the individual is inviolate, and the state has no authority and no interest other than that of assuring him the opportunity to enjoy those rights.

But immediately his activities intrude on the sphere of the rights of others, these activities become the business of the state.

I do not mean his potential activities. It is a sophistry, fascist in essence, that a man should be restrained because he might be dangerous.

Following this argument, a man should be restrained for any reason, on anybody's judgment.

This is simply placing unlimited power in the hands of the state. All that is not forbidden is compulsory. This is the ultimate conclusion of such a dogma.

It is plain history that those high-principled laws restraining potential treason, immorality, blasphemy, heresy, *ad nauseam*, lead inevitably to the star chamber and the concentration camp.

And censorship in any form is the opening wedge for fascism, since it places arbitrary and unwarranted power in the hands of individuals.

Titles and offices are only the labels of men; popes, presidents, judges and preachers are only men, like you and I.

And it is not good to place arbitrary power over the lives and opinions of men in the hands of men.

This has been amply demonstrated by history, ancient, medieval and modern. Such power is always abused. It has inevitably been used to gain further power—political, economic or spiritual.

And of these abusers the high-principled man is the most dangerous.

You will not get yourself shot to help line my pockets; but if I can convince you it is for the public good or the glory of God, that may be another matter.

This much for his potential actions. But when his activities include a control over the prices of rents, foods, light, power and other necessities, over laws, over expression in print or in public—or any other form of individual life, liberty and the pursuit of happiness—then his business most certainly becomes the business of the state.

The trend towards monopoly is one of the greatest dangers inherent in private enterprise. This trend must be circumvented by public controls.

When the press, the radio and the motion pictures are controlled by a small group, freedom of speech is inevitably curtailed and imperiled, as it is today.

The accumulation of undue power—whether by government, labor, religion or capital or by any other group—must be prevented at all costs. Freedom cannot survive the alternative.

Liberty will be always insecure until we realize this one fact. It simply does not matter who has the power, or in what name it is exercised.

The possession or exercise of undue power—whether it be the power to ostracize, to starve, to threaten and terrorize, to restrict and inhibit, to censor and deny—by any group and for any purpose, is always wrong.

The adequate restriction of power is the bulwark of civilization.

It is no part of the function of the state to enter competitively or solely into any business. A state monopoly is as undesirable and reprehensible as any monopoly.

But it is the function of the state to rigorously supervise and regulate all such activities, in order that those powers are not abused.

It is certain that graft and stupidity will enter into this supervision, at least until the public demands officials of a much higher caliber than the present.

It is certain that men will err. But it is better that some men have a limited power in order that other men do not have an unlimited power.

The rights and responsibilities of labor and capital are no more and no less than those of any other individual or group. Neither of these groups, or any other group, has any right whatever to use economic, political or social pressure, or violence or intimidation, against any other group or individual.

Those who do so must be held strictly accountable, by law and by the rights of man.

This, and not counter-violence and intimidation, is the proper recourse of opposing groups.

When this law breaks down, the citizens' committee is still bound by it, as a temporary state. If they are not, they are no more than a criminal mob.

This by no means denies the validity or the necessity of revolution in extreme cases.

When the state decays or collapses, or when the state or groups within the state arbitrarily violate the rights of individuals or other groups, and when all other recourse fails, then revolution becomes a necessity and a duty.

By revolution I mean an armed uprising designed to end tyranny, oppression and exploitation.

But this revolution, to be significant, must be inspired and guided by the principles of liberalism. Such was the American Revolution. But the Terror in France was a criminal mob. And the terror in Germany was an organized criminal mob.

There are vast differences.

The persecuted—the Negro, the Jew, the underprivileged—are fair game for tyrants who would woo them to their cause by a sentimental exploitation of their ignominy.

And such persons, understandably driven to fury or despair by their intolerable treatment, never stop to think that these tyrants itch to impose the same persecutions on other groups in other names.

To avail, a revolution must be something more than an inversion. Such persons, beyond all others, should understand liberalism and tolerance.

Persecutors and exploiters lurk behind names, institutions and traditions, often ridiculous and outworn, that receive the lip-service of the unthinking.

The greatest of the race are betrayed; the finest principles are smirched, perverted into wretched booby-traps.

Liberalism cannot substitute for liberals, and unless its code is informed by their blood, it will decay, as it has, and become infested, as it is.

The plutocrat, the demagogue and the shyster thrive in the carcass of a system splendidly designed to make men free. And the positivist haunts the aromatic vicinity like a jackal, seeking the moment when he may take advantage of the decay to appropriate the corpse.

Liberalism must be inspired with new life with each new generation. It must be reconstituted, restored and reaffirmed, lest, in a moment of quiescence, the carrion eaters close in.

But while man is a private individual, no group and no state have any right to the smallest moment of his time or the least fraction of his life. All service must be voluntary. All involuntary service is slavery, whitewash it as you will.

Both the closed shop and compulsory military conscription are clear violations of this precept. Certainly man has the right to join labor unions, to strike individually or *en masse* in order to obtain his objectives. But he must not be compelled to do so. No issue is of sufficient importance to warrant such a violation of individual liberty.

The case is similar with military conscription. This is a most flagrant violation of freedom. Certainly the individual may enlist in military service; under certain conditions it may be his duty. But he must not be compelled to do so. No state and no government has the right to force an individual to fight or die for its survival. No state and no issue is that important. I cannot force my neighbor to fight my battles; why should a coalition of my neighbors compel me to fight theirs? The use of force is never justified, except in self-defense or the defense of our principles, and we must not *compel* others to fight our battles.

The maintenance of world order is the proper function of a world state, which should maintain a properly armed police force for this purpose. Nations are as responsible as individuals—and, in fact, much more responsible. It is a minimum requirement of civilization that they be held strictly accountable for their acts.

In the absence of this minimum safeguard, honorable nations can only depend upon the voluntary enlistment of their citizens.

A state so dependent upon the affection and loyalty of its citizen for defense, would be most likely to cherish his liberties.

It should be a primary tenet of a world state that no nation can compulsorily conscript any person. The maintenance of national and world order should depend on persons voluntarily hired and properly paid for their services, as should be the case of any other police force.

A system in which a man is rudely torn from his home, family and business, paid a miserable pittance, and subjected to the insults and orders of a semi-fascist military, is insufferable and barbarous. It cannot be tolerated in a world dedicated to liberalism and democracy; it must not be tolerated by liberals.

Further, developments in modern warfare obviate the necessity for a large army. A world state is the only answer to the atom bomb. In the absence of this, the nations might as well let their citizens live the few remaining years left in peace and freedom. In the absence of this, in another ten years it won't make any difference.

Another most insidious totalitarian technique is universal military training. In the first place, like conscription, it is a clear violation of individual rights. In the second, it exposes youth, at its most impressionable and fanatical age, to indoctrination by the state. The youth training program is the foremost concern of every fascist and communist state.

So long as the military remains a necessary evil, it may be needful to maintain it with voluntary enlistment. If the inducements are adequate, the enlistment will be sufficient. But let us avoid even the shadow of compulsion, lest we find ourselves crushed by the substance.

III

The Sword and the Serpent

Of all the strange and terrible powers among which we move unknowingly, sex is the most potent.

Conceived in the orgasm of life, we burst forth in agony and ecstasy from the center of creation. Time and again we return to that fountain, lose ourselves in the fires of being, united for a moment with the eternal force, and return renewed and refreshed as from a miraculous sacrament. Then, at the last, our life closes in the orgasm of death.

Sex, typified as love, is at the heart of every mystery, at the center of every secret. It is this splendid and subtle serpent that twines about the cross, and coils in the core of the mystic rose.

The secret and the shame of Christianity is known when it is realized that the holy ghost is feminine—the Sophia. That is the true and natural order, father, mother, son. The very name of God, *yod he vau hé*—father, mother, son, daughter—when properly pronounced, asserts the splendor of the biological order. How could life proceed from a strictly masculine creation? What miracle could possibly be superior to the miracle of copulation, conception and gestation?

In the corrupt and demonic Jehova, the priesthood blasphemed nature in order to perpetuate a tyrannical and superstitious patriarchy.

Woman was insulted and affronted with the calumny of immaculate conception. Then, by this mystery-mongering, a premium hypnosis has been the basis of the power of the Church, and this is the source of so much of the psychosis rampant in the modern world.

It has been asserted that the church has been a champion of progress and freedom. Nothing could be more fallacious. Organized Christianity has been inevitably allied with tyranny, reaction, and persecution.

No organized dogma can contribute to progress, except accidentally. The church's one contribution has been to unintentionally foment revolt against its bigotry. It could hardly be otherwise with an organization founded on a double fallacy, the sin of sex and the infallibility of a man.

Nor can any other religion hope to benefit humanity while it preaches love and reviles the root of love. Anyone hoping to understand and cope with human relations must understand both the importance and the over-emphasis of sex in the human role.

Sex worship and sex symbolism are the basis of all the world's religions. Sex has been the source of the power of the organized Christian Church. Sex and sex neurosis are fundamental factors in the attitude of modern men. These three facts give sex a place of prime importance in the liberal examination of society.

Our sex attitudes are largely characterized by pretense. The majority of people under fifty today have engaged, at one time or another, in what is termed illicit intercourse, an unflattering label for a pleasant pastime.

Yet we pretend that we have not done so, we don't believe in it, never would do it, and disapprove very highly of the criminal types who do.

Policemen arrest and judges convict persons discovered in a pursuit which they themselves indulge at every opportunity.

Society, in the interims between its so-called adulteries and fornications, applauds the convictions.

The joyous (I hope) indulgence of a natural urge is defined as a crime. Young persons enjoying themselves, or trying to do so, are burdened with a sense of guilt and shame. They are classed with common criminals, with robbers and murderers.

Why?

The answer is shameful. Because at one time, in the dark ages, in conditions of squalor and misery, of filth, ignorance, superstition and oppression, the sex taboo was a prime instrument of power.

It was the instrument of power of a fascistic, murderous, sadistic group of brigands known as the Christian Church.

This is the reason that today young persons in love are classed as criminals, venereal disease thrives, and abortionists prosper.

The superstition which fostered this shameful thing is no longer absolutely dominant. But the vile instrument of its power, that horror that termed the human body indecent, love obscene, that fouled women with the infamy of original sin and insulted her with the implied calumny of immaculate conception, that filthy thing remains to mold our thoughts and shape our laws.

It is most significant that the spiritual and physical inheritors of that church, both Catholic and Protestant, vigorously and effectively oppose birth control, venereal disease information, divorce laws, and in short, anything which would impose any limitation on that ignorance and savagery which is their chief power. Nor is this obscenity palliated by the fact that the dupes are sincere. To deny the dissemination of contraceptive techniques and information to persons who do not desire or cannot afford a family; to prevent public instruction on sex, and sex hygiene; and to thereby foment and abet abortion, syphilis and untold misery—all in the name of an indemonstrable superstition, a supernatural taboo; this is the charity of the church.

To maintain at all costs every king, tyrant, and fascist dictator who supports the status quo against a popular government; such is her mercy.

To prevent by every possible trick the free discussion or exposition of sex and religion in art, literature, and education, that is her justice.

If such groups limited this folly to their own believers, they would be within their rights. Man has the right to any personal stupidity, however monstrous it may seem.

But this is not their principal concern. They seek to impose this nonsense on everybody, by every means of legal, moral, and economic domination and intimidation in their control.

The success of this program can be judged by the state of the press, the radio, the motion pictures and the law. Then, true to form and fascist as always, the censor utilizes his moral victory to impose political and social censorships in all fields. Bigots and demagogues invoke the divine right of religion and of morality in order to gain extraordinary power.

But neither freedom of religion nor of the press can be used as a dodge to suppress freedom in those and other fields. We must not only have freedom of religion; we must have freedom from religion.

The concept that sex in art, literature and life is subject to criminal law is based on the superstitious religious-sexual taboo. The censorial power of the church, the state and the yellow press is founded solely on this one assumption: that the taboo of a special religion has legal sanction.

And this sanction, once established, is then subtly extended to all the sacred social and political creeds and dogmas of that religion.

Thus religion, always respectable and conservative, forms alliances with fascist and capitalist cliques, which then have free sanction to persecute and propagandize against liberalism in all its forms. This unholy alliance is thus free to commit any excess of chicanery and censorship, under the name of freedom of religion and the press.

When ninety percent of the press, the radio, and the film industry is thus dominated by a small clique, the type of freedom to be expected can be easily defined.

Superstition, taboo, reaction and fascism augment one another marvelously. Nor is the fact that one type of totalitarianism persecutes another—or appears to do so—any palliative.

Modern man must recognize the source and nature of his sexual taboos, and destroy them at their source. Only thus can he achieve sanity in sex, and, through this, sanity in all living.

In this society, early marriages are often prevented by economic considerations. Beyond all this, premarital sexual relations are natural, and very often desirable.

Contraceptive techniques, available to any intelligent young person from druggist or doctor, can minimize the problem of venereal disease and premature offspring.

The development of sex technique, the determination of the qualifications of a partner, the gratification of the youthful urge to experimentation, all assure a far more lasting and stable marriage than one begun in ignorance and prudery.

In marriage itself the social contract is binding, and property by the joint efforts of husband and wife belongs to both jointly. Where any two persons have pledged their love together, no outsider has the right to interfere, and either party is justified in resisting such interference, by force if necessary.

But neither party, whether the relationship be in or out of wedlock, has any right or jurisdiction over the love or affection, the body or sex life, of another for longer than that other desires.

Where children are concerned, and a separation is desired, a serious problem is always encountered. A broken home is hard on a child. A loveless and bitter home is worse. No state can assure a child the affection of his parents. But a state can guarantee his physical welfare and security, and thus insure him against many of the frustrations of childhood and adolescence, which develop unstable and maladjusted adults.

The laws against mutually agreeable sex expression must be repealed, together with laws prohibiting nudism and birth control, and sex censorship laws.

We must emphatically and positively deny that love is criminal and that the body is indecent. We must affirm the beauty, the dignity, the humor and the joyousness of sex.

Indeed, there are obscene things in the light and in the darkness, things that deserve destruction.

And among these things are the exploitation of women for a miserable wage, the shameful degradation of minorities by the foul little lice that call themselves members of a superior race, and the deliberate and malicious machinations towards war.

But nowhere among those things is the love that is between a man and a woman, or between a boy and a girl.

There are sins, but love is not one of them. But of all the things that have been called sins, love has been the most punished and the most persecuted. Of all the things we know, the springtime of love is closest to paradise. And as all things pass, love passes—too soon.

This most exquisite and tender of human emotions—why should it not be free, for its little moment of eternity? Why should it be bought and sold, chained and restricted, until lovers, caught in the maelstrom of economics and law, are hounded like criminals?

What end is served, and who profits, by such cruelty? Only priests and lawyers.

Let us adhere to a strict morality where the rights and happiness of our fellow man is concerned. Let us call our true sins by their right names, and expiate them accordingly.

But let our lovers go free.

If we are to achieve civilization and sanity, we must institute an educational program in love-making, birth control, and disease prevention, in order to circumvent frustration, abortion and syphilis.

Above all, we must root out the barbaric and vicious concepts of shamefulness and indecency in sex, and expose the techniques and motives of their proponents.

Happy are the parents who, as a result of sexual experiments, are well mated; who take joy in each other's passion, in their bodies, in each other's nakedness; who do not fear to expose these bodies or the bodies of their children; who do not shame or inhibit their children's joy in sex play. And happy are the children of such parents.

And one word for the "fallen" woman. Jesus, who was a god, said "Go, and sin no more." But I, who am a man, say to you who have given with exquisite joy and pleasure without thought of gain or recompense, who have given your body for the need of man's body, who have given your love freely for his spirit's sake: "Be blessed in the name of man. And if any god deny you for this, I will deny that god."

The ancients, being simple and without original sin, saw God in the act of love. And therein they saw a great mystery, a sacrament revealing the bounty and the beauty of the force that made men and the stars. And thus they worshipped.

Poor ignorant old pagans—how we have progressed. We see a dirty joke.

And from this horrible and sordid joke only woman herself can redeem us. She who has been its ignominious butt, the target of malice and arrogance, the target of masculine inferiority and guilt, she alone can redeem us from our crucifixion and castration.

Only woman, of and by herself, can strike through the foolish frustration of the advertisers' ideal, and rise, her strong, free splendid self, to take her place in the sun as an individual, a companion, a mate fit for and demanding no less than a true man.

Let there be an end to inhibition and an end to pretense. Let us discover what we are, and be what we are, honestly and unashamedly.

The rabbit has speed to recompense his fear, and the panther strength to assuage his hunger. There is room for both; perhaps the rabbit would prefer a world of rabbits, but it would be very dull, soon overpopulated and foodless.

All things are good—wrath, fear, lust, laziness—if they are balanced by strength and intelligence.

While we lie about the things we call our weaknesses and sins, while we say that this is evil and that is wrong, and falsely deny that such a thing could be in us, these things will grow crooked in the dark.

But have them out in the open, admit them, face them, accept them, and we will be ashamed to have them remain crippled and twisted.

Then fear can sharpen our wits against adversity, anger and strength can be welded into a sword against tyrants within and without, and lust can be trained to be the strong and subtle servant of love and art.

It is not necessary to deny anything. It is only necessary to know ourselves. Then we will naturally seek that which is needful to our being, and reject that which is alien to it. But this can only be done by experience.

Our significance does not lie in the extent to which we resemble others, or in the extent to which we differ from them. It lies within our ability to be ourselves, and this may well be the entire object of life — to discover ourselves, our meaning. But this cannot be some sudden burst of illumination. It is a constant process, which continues so long as we are truly alive.

This process cannot continue unobstructed unless we are free to undergo all experience, and willing to participate in all of existence. Then the significant questions are not "is it right" or "is it good," but rather "how does it feel" and "what does it mean."

Ultimately, these are the only sort of questions that can approach any sort of truth. But they cannot be asked in the absence of freedom.

There was a time when these questions were whispered in the shadow of the stake. That Christian instrument of conversion is not sanctioned at present, but the will and the malice remain and will remain until the power of the superstitious taboo is finally broken. Meanwhile, the religious dogma continues to enforce the sexual jealousies of psychotic parents for their children, and psychotic marriage partners for their mates.

It is not alone because of economic desperation and greed that crime and war wash over the world in ever-mounting waves. It is only necessary to look to the middle ages, when, in three successive generations, St. Vitus' dance, epilepsy and syphilis—benighted horrors of Christian guilt and shame—swept the western world. It was this frightfulness as well as the corrupt and stupid policies of the western empires that produced the liberal revolutions of the eighteenth century. But the root, the sexual taboo, was unfortunately not destroyed, and remained to revitalize the power of religion over the new bourgeoisie.

The frenetic hatred of Jews and Negroes (symbols of illicit sexual freedom), and the lust toward the blood- and fire-baths of war, are the very abattoirs of sexual frustration, the nightmares of souls in a hell of guilty desire. They labor like madmen over their instruments of destruction in order to kill the world and die in the holocaust. It is only in the unobstructed exercise of the sexual function, by a generation trained from youth in contraception and the technique of love, that it will be possible to come to a mature social relation.

In this childish folly of sexual possession, each man and each woman hates and fears every other man and woman as the potential despoiler or inhibitor of his sex life. The marriage relation is turned into a gruesome joke by the ever-present specters of jealousy and suspicion.

It is curious to note that the entire problem is resolved by the application of two old axioms: "that you love one another," and "that you do unto others as you would have others do unto you."

The application of these maxims in the sexual sphere is easy and pleasant, and firmly established thus, it may spread to other spheres.

The sexual revolution will not produce any instantaneous paradise, nor will it be accomplished without tears. The way to racial maturity is long and painful, and we, children and savages all, cannot imagine its end. It may be hastened by individual effort, but such effort is in the main thankless; the rewards, if any, are of the interior sort. If it is possible to attain, in private life, the maturity and richness that comes with full and satisfactory sexual expression, that is sufficient. It may be that other considerations are of more importance in extreme age, but I would hesitate to say what age would be that extreme. Certainly, it does not seem possible to grow old gracefully unless one has known something of a graceful youth.

IV
The Sword and the Spirit

There is no evidence to show that man is created and accoutered to serve as God's viceregent upon the earth. There is no reason to believe that he is naturally good and kind and brave and wise, or ever was. On the contrary, there is much to show that he is a beast that has taken a strange turning in the jungle, and blundered rather aimlessly into a mental world in which he is certainly not at home.

There is much evidence that he is by nature cruel, cowardly, lustful, avaricious and treacherous, and he holds dominion against these terrible internal enemies, and against the other predators, by virtue of his ferocity, his cunning, and his indomitable will.

This is his beauty and his significance: that out of the blind primordial forces of sex and survival he has forged reason and science, and spun the gossamer splendors of art and love.

If there is no other reason and no other significance, man himself has on occasion created reason and significance, and stood, maker of gods, in a garden made fruitful by his own creative power.

We think in terms of ourselves relative to the external universe. It cannot be shown, however, that this external universe is other than an extension of our perception. But even if we differ, the internal from the external, we are part of, and not separate from, the entire process of nature. We are made from the nova by way of the sun, and built from the air and the rock and the sea, and the primordial fire of life. There are filaments in our consciousness that reach back to the first ancestor, and extend to all other men, and to all other life, with which we share a common creation and a common destiny.

Here is the totality, that the Greeks called Pan, all-devourer, all-begetter, life and death, good and evil, pain and pleasure, unity, duality, multiplicity, all things beyond all things, the soul of night and the stars. If in our folly and fear we will ascribe moral qualities to the lightning that strikes, to the star that shines, to the tiger that kills, then we will not hesitate to assign them also to the woman that gives and the man that takes, define God, and found a religion.

Thus we degrade the living universe into a bewhiskered and irascible character endowed with immortality, and a hatred for our enemies. Or, with those nature lovers who catch cold, or babies communing with the all in the park at night, we fearfully retire into the platitudinous sitz baths of Christian Science or Unity, or frenziedly embrace a cause, all on the way to the fear-frozen catalepsy of middle age.

All nature partakes of the eternal sacraments of life and death, of ebb and flow, of creation and destruction and regeneration. These are the harmonies of eternity that change forever and never change. The cry of a baby is echoed in the tumult of the novae. Men, suns and seasons pass, and return again. The spate of semen is one with the jet of stars men call the Milky Way.

The mind that comprehends these immortal processes in love and in worship is an immortal mind, that soars beyond time and death. We are of one age with Aeschylus and Sophocles and Shakespeare, of one blood with Moses and Lao-tzu and Newton. The body changes and decays; time cuckolds all shapes of desire, all transient things.

But the shapes of desire, although transient, are the very vehicles of man's adventure; he cannot attain by denying these steeds, but by strengthening them, by training and bridling with love and creative will until the wings are revealed.

Sex and hunger are the raw stuff of art, and out of his passion and fury and despair the artist transmutes the shapes of terror and wonder into an eternal beauty.

So can each desire, and each requirement be transmuted, by love and devotion, into an availing aspiration.

All ways are the right way when will and love are the guides, and the grace and bounty of life are free to all—saint and sinner alike—who desire it.

The voice of the wind, the poignancy of music, the shout of thunder call man to dare; to know himself. Sunlight and sea and stars, and the splendor of a naked woman, are the signs and witnesses of a covenant that is forever.

And we know these things—know them with the only certainty that is ever given us. This is the beautiful pitiable knowledge of childhood and first youth, that the world denies, and necessity circumvents.

This is the knowledge of the poets and artists and singers, that are beloved and outcast by men; and of the mystics, that the world call mad.

And man, self-castrated and self-frustrated, flees down the corridors of nightmares, pursued by monstrous machines, overwhelmed by Satanic powers, haunted by vague guilts and terrors—all created of his own imagination.

He escapes into absurdity, drowns his spirit in pretense, worships brass gods of power and tin gods of success. Then, shamed by his pretenses and frustrated by his self-denial, he frenziedly projects his horror on imagined enemies, seeks release in scapegoats and false issues, and propitiates these anthropoid gods, the blackened and shattered eidolons of his spirit, with sacrifices of blood.

Nothing is of its nature evil, and nothing is of its nature good. Evil is only excess, good is simply balance. All things are subject to abuse; all things are susceptible to beneficial use. And balance does not consist in denial, or excess of indulgence. Balance can only be obtained by exceeding. These are the powers in man's nature, so tremendous that they can only be balanced by an ultimate self-expression.

To place limitations and restrictions on this nature is to build a wall of plaster around a sun. It is to clip the eagle's wings, to feed carrots to a lion. He will die or turn monstrous; he will not be uplifted or improved. The fundamental purpose of religion is to attain an identity with a power which we believe to be greater than ourselves, whose omnipotence and immortality we can share. Then, having achieved some sense of this identity, we feel that we can cope with problems, and attain ends which would otherwise defeat us. The reliance on religion as well as the reliance on property, is a lack of self-reliance.

It is ourself that creates this god of power; it is ourself from which his power is drawn; and this self is greater than any god which it creates. Therefore, to know ourselves is the highest form of wisdom, and to believe in ourselves is the highest form of faith. Science, which seeks to know, and art, which seeks to interpret, are two forms of love, which is the only available way of worship; and that these two greatest expressions of the human spirit should be subservient to religion, politics, nationalism and war is the craziest blasphemy that has been perpetuated on the race.

We are now in the midst of a tremendous battle of forces contending for domination over the mind and spirit of man, and it is not, unfortunately, a battle between good and evil, between freedom and tyranny, but a struggle of dogma with dogma, and authority with authority. The major contenders are fascism and communism. Each is a doctrine alien and hostile to the ideal of freedom. Each says that we must choose between one and the other; and each is, in reality, identical, the one with the other. Each demands the absolute enslavement of the individual, the abnegation of the intellect, and the subjugation of the will.

The authoritarian is right, absolutely right, so right that every extreme of falsehood, suppression, and tyranny is justified in accomplishing his divine ends. And behind his benevolence, his inevitabilities, is the ever-present star chamber and concentration camp; the rack, the stake, and the inquisition of the much-lamented old time religion. All of these systems are old, as old as history, as old as slavery and murder and human misery and despair. Freedom and democracy are the only new things under the sun, and they offend alike the slaves and the slave masters. "Come unto me," goes the old harlot song, "come unto me you weary and heavily laden, surrender this intolerable burden of freedom and I will fill your mouths with miracles and your bellies will be full of food. Come with me, and I will confound your enemies and show you paradise. Look, you do not even have to change a name, only keep the letter and deny the spirit, for the letter giveth life." She is harvesting the nations now, that old whore, for an appointment in the place called Armageddon.

There will be a hunting of free men in the name of freedom, and there will be prisons and pogroms in the name of democracy, and murder and slavery in the name of brotherhood, all for the sake of dominion over the minds and bodies of men.

But there is a choice. There is the choice of freedom, which has no other name and no other cause. Man, freed of his demons, without the need of a dogma or the use of a creed, can of and by himself, through untrammeled experience, avail, triumph, and achieve significance. This is the faith of a liberal: belief in himself and belief in man. There is no other way to the full stature of manhood. It is the long way, the hard way—through trial and error, failure, heartbreak and despair. But it is a way—guided by science and inspired by art—which leads, at long last, to the stars.

This is our choice. We may believe in ourselves, believe in our fellow men, and, in freedom and in brotherhood, start to achieve, here and now that paradise which has so long been relegated to the hereafter. Or with the dogmatists, the positivists, the authoritarians—feudal fascists all—we can return again to the full apehood from which we are so late arisen.

If we wish identity with a greater power, let us seek a union with ourself—our total self raised to its highest potential of wisdom, knowledge and experience. If we wish to unite with the universe, let us court the whole of nature—all experience, all truth—the wonder and the terror, the splendor and the pity and the pain of the awesome cosmos itself.

For out there lies the great campaign that comes first and last, the ultimate adventure of the individual into himself. He must go—down like Moses, into his unknown self; out into the new dimension; out with Orpheus and the barque of Arthur, with Tammuz, and Adonis, with Mithra and Jesus—into the labyrinths of the dark land. There he will meet the Mother, and hear her final question—which is not a silly riddle, but the most wonderful and terrible of all questions: "what is man?"

And thereafter, close by the heart of the cryptic Mother, he may find the Graal: ultimate consciousness, total remembrance, instinct made certain, reason made real. For it is he, wonderful monster, embryo god, that has swum in the fish, shed the skin of the crocodile, peered from the eyes of serpents, swung with the ape, and shaken the earth with the tramp of the tyrannosaur's hoof. It is he who has cried out on all crosses, ruled on all thrones, grubbed in all gutters. It is he whose face is reflected and distorted in all heavens and hells; he, the child of the stars, the son of the ocean; this creature of dust, this wonder and terror called man.

V

Sword Play

In the preceding chapters, I have examined liberalism and liberal principles and drawn certain conclusions. Among the most salient are these:

There is no sound basis for dogmatism or positivism on any subject. Truth is relative. There is no justification for compulsion or restriction in the individual's private sphere.

All men have certain basic rights in the sphere of private thought, action and self-expression. No state and no group has any right to supersede these rights.

When men's actions intrude on the rights of other men, these actions are subject to regulation by the state.

The state exists for the primary purpose of protecting the rights of the individual. It is possible to deduce a philosophy commensurate with the principles of liberalism, and informing these principles with a more than social significance.

I can deduce no gaseous god that is separate and apart from man, and no continuous and halcyon hereafters. There is no demonstrable reason for a superstitious observance of any sort—of the church, of the state, of law, morals, or dogma. But there is much in man that is worthy of worship; there is that in humanity and nature that is divine. There is beauty in the world sufficient for any paradise, dreamed or imagined.

Thus, if there is no supernatural comfort in times of stress and danger, still there is will and courage, and manifestly have these servants of the least of men availed beyond all gods.

And if there is no supernal love in heaven, still there is love on earth—love enough for all, free to all who will and dare to the estate of the high art of life. It may be argued that this is a negative thesis throughout, and that no positive doctrine can be postulated on such a basis. That is exactly the conclusion. We must outgrow the need for dogmas which force us into a stultified and mechanical relation with life, and live by and for a continuous and vital experience, interpreted and made significant by the creative mind. It may appear from such considerations that here is a difficult and hazardous way of life.

This is true, and it has always been true. Life itself requires the highest courage.

Jesus was a liberal, one of the most dangerous who ever lived. He denied the church, preaching the personal and interior nature of the kingdom of heaven. He denied the authority of the state and the home, preaching the higher allegiance to individual conscience.

Had his philosophy succeeded, it would have overthrown the Jewish religion and the Roman state.

To circumvent him, it was first necessary to kill him and all those of his followers with understanding, and afterwards to subvert his teachings into another do-as-you-are-told soothing syrup.

The first goal was achieved by the contemporary state, and the second by the Christian Church.

In a similar manner, modern liberals have been persecuted, and their philosophies subverted, by fascists and communists, by patriots and zealots, throughout the world. And the most efficient destroyers have been their own followers, who trampled on the spirit and crucified the spiritual inheritors.

The most powerful and wealthy groups are on the side of reaction and tyranny, and supported by every trick of propaganda that can influence a slavish public opinion and mass indifference.

The most violent and radical groups are on the side of revolution and tyranny. Both of these groups usurp the name of liberalism to gain their despicable ends, and castigate the true liberal who is caught between these two maelstroms.

The liberal will find himself opposed and thwarted by the church, the press and the law—and by public opinion itself. He will be called a crank, cheat, visionary and a fool. Over and over the cries of "communism," "fascism," and "atheism"—those modem counterparts of treason and heresy—will be raised by the witch hunter, the bigot and the yellow journalist. Such are the watchwords of intimidation and blackmail.

He will seek for organizations in which he can express himself, and find these organizations only too willing to subvert his principles for their own gain. If he lives his belief, he will often find himself opposed even by his family and his friends. But he cannot accept defeat simply because the battle is difficult. He will realize the enormous power of the forces entrenched against him, and the almost insurmountable difficulty of accomplishing even the slightest gain.

But he will also realize his incalculable debt to the champions of freedom before him, who have paid with blood for the little liberty he has. And he will understand his responsibility to them, to himself and to his fellows, and the terrible need the world has for him, for whatever little he can do. The battle for freedom is not fought alone on the great fronts. It is fought in every home, in every community, in every state in the world. It is fought in the mind and heart of every man.

Where there is an artist or scientist struggling to express his dream, to be true to himself; where there is an underprivileged man, an exploited worker, a bond slave of the military, a man bullied by unions or harried by dictators—there is the battle for freedom. Where there is a child intimidated, a woman enslaved; where the ignorant and credulous are exploited by religion—there is the fight. And where a boy and girl are hunted and hounded because they love—draw the sword there.

There is no lack of issues. Freedom is always an issue.

This is no reason to butt into the private affairs of others, to chase red herrings at full cry, or otherwise to make a fool of oneself yapping about the "cause."

The sword is only worthy of those who will fight, and of those that have good reason to fight.

The battle plan of the liberal is simple. He can take a basic declaration of principles such as those outlined heretofore. He can regulate his own life by those principles and infuse them into his own work.

He can examine laws, groups, and activities in his community, his state and his nation in the light of these principles. Where he finds them violated, there is his fight.

He can cooperate with other individuals and groups who are even in partial accord with his principles and seek, without compromising his own ideas too much, to achieve at least some small gain.

He must learn to concentrate on limited objectives. He can easily find one law, one group, one activity which is in flagrant violation of human rights and human dignity. He can attack this with publicity, with petition, and with agitation. He will find that others will help him gain this freedom if he will help them in their sphere.

There is danger in all organization. But there are times when there is greater danger in the lack of organization. We face such a time. It is doubtful that the liberal can long survive the enormous power of groups devoted to his extinction. In the process of the last war, many freedoms were suppressed, and there is as yet no sign of their return.

There is constant and availing agitation for the conscription of labor, for the regimentation of business, and for the regulation and supervision of every form of private life.

Trends indicate the almost inevitable development of some form of state socialism. In view of the complex and disastrous forms of modem economics and sociology, this may be inevitable.

But even if the state must regulate the financial and economic life of the nation, it must not and cannot meddle with the private life of the individual.

If the liberal understands the differences and relations between these two spheres, he can achieve much for society and for freedom. If he does not, he will become the unwitting dupe of state slavery.

Equally ubiquitous and equally malevolent is the enemy within. We are enslaved as effectively by inhibition, by fear, by weakness as we ever are by the outward and more spectacular tyrants; and how mistaken we are to dismiss that which is the intangible, or encompassed in a small space. The atom is small, and the electron is intangible. The critical mass of plutonium is about three and one-half pounds, and the weight of a man's brain is not much more. What is the weight of a fertilized ovum, from which the mind arises?

Yet in that mind are encompassed mountains and plains and planets, nebulae and the universe of stars. Poetry and philosophy, mathematics and music flourish in this frail network of cells.

But no mind can long control the powers of nature that cannot control itself. The intellect may invoke demons from atoms and suns, but only the will can command them.

How long we have juggled the great elemental powers in careless arrogance. Fire and earth, air and water, the great archangels themselves have been the docile servitors of our greed, our malice, and our cowardice. And yet we do not understand or control these powers, even in ourselves.

The vengeance that these forces can take upon us — foolish apprentices without the wit to command or the wisdom to obey nature — may be a lesson for a future race.

It is within ourselves [that] the sword is forged that will avail us in outer battles. It is from the soul and mind and heart of the individual that the force is drawn that will transmute the race. In all the planes it is love alone that signifies, but love can signify nothing unless it is bastioned by will and courage. To even maintain liberty at a given status is a difficult task. To extend it is a heroic task. Our liberty is not maintained or extended by acquiescence or by talk. It is more comfortable to leave the defense and extension of freedom in the hands of those who are elected or paid for this purpose, but it is also more dangerous, as comfortable things often are. It is not easy to continuously fight or be ready to fight; to stay lean and hard against a necessity that is never very far away.

But this is exactly what is required if we are to even maintain our liberties in the condition in which we received them. The enemies of freedom are indefatigable and all the more deadly because power, prestige, habit and public inertia are on their side. Even those who find nonresistance comfortable may not find slavery comfortable, and slavery is the right name for regimentation, despite the euphemism its proponents may devise.

The time to fight for freedom is the time when freedom is threatened, not the time when freedom is destroyed, for that later time is too late. Freedom is threatened now; the destruction of freedom is not far off. Now is the time to fight.

VI

The Woman Girt with a Sword

It is to you, woman, beautiful lost redeemer of the race, that I dare address this chapter. That which stirs in you now is not madness, is not sin, is not folly, but is life, new life, and joy and fire that will beget a new race, and create a new heaven and a new earth. When you were a child, did not the wind speak to you and the sun? Did you not hear the mountain's voice, the voices of the river and the storm? Have you not heard the tidings of the stars, and the voices in the silence, ineffable?

Have you not gone naked in the forest, with the wind over your body, and felt the caress of Pan? And your heart has swelled with spring, blossomed with summer, and saddened with the wolf of winter. These things are the covenant, and in them is the truth that is forever.

And you have sought companions as high-hearted as yourself, and found them not, save in elusive memories in dream and song. For you found a blight over the world, a blight of silence and sorrow, and your companions walked in guilt and shame, in fear and hate, sin and the sorrow of sin, and you were alone. Ah, there was laughter, but a hectic laughter, pleasure but furtive pleasure, unsatisfied and ashamed. And now your heart is saddened. But be not sad, my beloved. Be joyous and unafraid. For within you is the song that shall shatter the silence, the flame that will burn away the dross.

It is you that are the redeemer, the redeemer of sin and sorrow, of guilt and shame—you, woman, oh splendor incarnate! How long have you served in chains, a slave to the lust of pigs and the guilt of pigs?

How long have you writhed under the foul degradation of your holy name, whore, or suffered silently under the infamous degradation called virtue?

How well have you known the stake, the rack, the whip, bar, chains, imprisonment, entombment in the service of your master.

And was the bond fear, was it weakness, was it cowardice and inferiority? Oh, shame of man, it was none of these — it was love. A man was crucified in a redemption that failed. Yet were ten times ten million men crucified, this infamy were not redeemed.

Priest, father, husband, lover, jailer, judge, executioner, despoiler, seducer, destroyer — this has been your lover, your master; oh, woman defiled.

Yet pity him, for he too sought love.

But there is an end, and a beginning, and the beginning and all the future is with you. For you are the mother of the new race, the redeemer and lover of the new men, the men that shall be free.

Now I shall speak to you of men. Men desire three things of woman: a mother greater than themselves, a wife less than themselves, and a lover equal with themselves. Against the mother they are ever in revolt, the wife they hold in contempt, the lover ever eludes them.

Consider the husband; how he hates woman and flees himself, fearing that he will slay her.

Consider the great lover; how he grasps for love, and his hands close upon nothingness.

These are bewildered, frightened children, playing games against the dark. And those who wear brass and swords, who strut and slay, are they not the most frightened of all? Therefore pity them; therefore forgive them.

In the ancient world there were men for a season; then cities arose, and leisure — the riddle of the sphinx — and they turned to gilded popinjays, gracefully accepting futility.

Then Christianity, an anodyne for slaves, an enteric for barbarians whose deeds gave them indigestion, a whip for slave masters.

Yes, Faust is the prototype of the middle ages, but not the Faustus of whom Kit Marlowe tells. It is a darker Faust, Gilles de Retz, who betrays the Maid in his lust for power; then, smitten, prays to God in his chapel, and ascends to all horror in his cellars.

And so the dreary story, until man, appalled by his own nightmares, turns at last to the dream of liberty.

It is the voice of Voltaire—jaded, cynical, weary of folly—that sounds the opening bar of a tremendous and mocking prelude; Tom Paine—one man, one real man, broken and at last betrayed by all the wooden champions; Cagliostro, plotting the revenge of the Templars with a woman and a necklace; Will Blake speaking uncomprehended, with the tongue of angels; Shelley and his beautiful futile gesture; Swinburne, that almost recreated Helas before he too was broken; Byron, Pushkin, Gautier—all instruments in a prelude to a symphony that was never played.

And science, how it was to save us. That brave new world of Huxley, Darwin, Hegel and H. G. Wells, with only the voice of Spengler to dissent. Science remaking the world, an international language, a universal brotherhood, beyond nationality or prejudice or creed. That house of cards, beautiful vision—how it has fallen. These creators of the new age, who dare not speak or think or move without permission of the military. Unboundaried titans, who will hang for speaking across one border, where is your new world? Champions, where is freedom? What has gone awry?

A man can guess but no man can solve. We must turn to woman for the answer.

It was many thousand years ago, before histories were written, that the change came. We must turn our memories even farther. Why can we not [remember], who sprang from those loins—though it be long ago, the age of Isis that is mistakenly called the matriarchy? It is not a matriarchy as we imagine it—a rule of clubwomen, or frustrated chickens. It is an equality. The woman is the priestess; in her reposes the mystery. She is the mother, brooding yet tender; the lover, at once passionate and aloof; the wife, revered and cherished. She is the witch woman. It is coequal, undifferentiated. The man—chieftain, hunter, husband, lover, thinker, doer. The woman—priestess, guardian of the mystery, sibyl of the unconscious, prophetess of dreams. Thus balance, stability.

Then, catastrophe untellable—the patriarchy, archetypified by the demonic monosexual monster, Jehova. And now, in the rule of priests, woman is an inferior animal, man a superior god; isolated, and at the mercy of his merciless intelligence. It is war, total war without quarter, between the emotions that must and the intellect that will not. Every religion in the patriarchy is a self-contradictory monstrosity—Judaism, Christianity, Buddhism, Mohammedism, fascism, communism, democracy, science and every other faith of the historical world. It is dogma—creed based on axioms that shift like straws in the wind of the intellect—and upon this shifting structure man has failed; and must fail, for he knows their futility, and fights for them with all the sick fury of frustration. He knows that he is a little boy playing with erector toys and chemical sets, playing cops and robbers in a game that goes too far.

He has lost his mother; his wife fails him; his lover eludes him. The mystery has gone out of the temple, banished by a senile and self-sufficient council of beards. Woman, woman, where are you? Come back, woman, come back to us again! Forgive, forget, sit in our temples, take us by the hand, kiss us on the lips, tell us that you love us, that we are not alone. Witch woman, out of the ashes of the stake, rise again!

You see, it was in the Dianic cult that the old way continued. Those splendid and terrible women—Messalina, Toffana, La Voisin and De Brinvilliers—took magnificent revenges. And other women—and men too—sought the forbidden mystery in secret rites, and purchased a brief reunion at an awful price.

This was the hope in the maid of Orleans, the hope of hopeless millions that at last was come the woman who would redeem them. May her fate and her failure teach you that innocence is no protection.

Be cunning, oh woman; be wise, be subtle, be merciless. I have said: understand, forgive, forget. But forget not overmuch. Trust nothing but yourself.

I have spoken of those great poisoners, but there is a worse revenge. Know that all revenge is revenge on self, and most terrible is that taken by the frigid woman. Count her in the millions and in the ten millions. Heed not what she tells her husband or lover, heed well what she tells her intimate, her doctor.

But with many the cause lies deeper. It lies in two things: the failure of her mate to be a man, and her failure to be true to herself.

There is the black murderous guilt with which parents poison their children, and that is a cause of frigidity.

There is suppressed incestuous love.

There is fear of disease, and of children.

But you, who have known something of these things, have no shame therefore. Strength is not born, it is gained by understanding and overcoming.

Then go free! Then sing the old, wild song: EVOE IO, EVOE IACCHUS IO PAN IO PAN EVOE BABALON!

Go to the mountains and the oceans and the forest, go naked in the summertime, that you may regain the old joy, and love gladly and freely under the stars.

But the body is not beautiful? Here is a secret. The body is molded by the mind. Embrace fear, repression, hate; then look upon the body—or rather do not look upon it. But go free; love joyously, without restraint; run naked a little. Then watch the cheeks flush; see the breasts swell—the supple contours, the flowing rhythm. All disease and all deformity are bred in fear and hate. Therefore, oh woman, are you called healer.

Woman, priestess of the irrational world! Irrational, but enormously important, and how deadly because it is unadmitted and denied.

We do not want to be drunken, murderous, frustrated, poverty-stricken, miserable without cause. These things are not reasonable or scientific; yet they do exist. We say we do not want war. But the cause of war is a psychological necessity, and war will continue until that necessity is otherwise fulfilled.

We do not avail in saying that we will love this person, or hate that person, because it is reasonable. We are moved willy-nilly, despite our reason, and our will forces, out of the unconscious, irrational world—forces that speak to us in dreams, in symbols, and in our own incomprehensible actions, and that would only be redeemed by understanding, whose name is woman. Only after understanding can will and intelligence prevail, for they are otherwise no more than blind, self-destructive force.

Woman, put up unworthy weapons. Put up malice and poison, false frigidity and false stupidity. Draw the sword, the two-edged sword of freedom, and call for a man to meet you in fair combat, a man fit for your husband, fit father for your eagle brood.

Call upon him; test him by the sword, and he will be worthy of you. For you two are the archetypes of the new race. Somewhere in the world today there is a woman for whom the sword is forged. Somewhere there is one who has heard the trumpets of the new age, and who will respond. She will respond, this new woman, to the high clamor of those star trumpets; she will come as a perilous flame and a devious song, a voice in the judgment halls, a banner before armies. She will come girt with the sword of freedom, and before her kings and priests will tremble and cities and empires will fall, and she will be called BABALON, the scarlet woman. For she will be lustful and proud; she will be subtle and deadly, she will be forthright and invincible as a naked blade. And women will respond to her war cry, and throw off their shackles and chains, and men will respond to her challenge, forsaking the foolish ways and the little ways, and she who will shine as the ruddy evening star in the bloody sunset of Götterdamerung, will shine again as a morning star when the night has passed, and a new dawn breaks over the garden of Pan.

To you, oh unknown woman, [is] the sword pledged. Keep the faith!

DOING YOUR WILL

Doing Your Will

I

Tonight I will attempt to present you with the outline of a practical reduction of the philosophy behind *The Book of the Law*, as it applies to our modern life.

This will be difficult, since there is an enormous background of technical, historical, social, and psychological data which I shall be forced to omit. This is all available. I hope that you will be sufficiently interested to review it yourself, if you have not done so.

If you will remember that I am dealing with the end product of this material, and trying, in a very short period, to condense this into a practical conclusion, I will appreciate your tolerance.

There are certain individuals who aspire to a maximum of independence, in thought and in action, in order to achieve the optimum in the function of their nature and their creative Will.

From among such have come the dreamers and creators, the leaders and revolutionaries, artists and poets and scientists. All that we know of progress and of culture has come from them; all, out of the neolithic swamp, by fire and air, by earth and water, and by the creative word, has come from those minds, from those hands.

The anthropoid mind fears and mistrusts such sorts, and rides, an unwilling ape, on the coat-tails of the creative evolute. Unwilling, unwitting, and often something more than that.

In the indomitable Will of the first order genius, there is sufficient ferocity or subtlety to overcome arboreal opposition, although the manifest result is usually post mortem, over a somewhat mutilated corpse.

But there are numberless fine minds—men and women of high talent and culture—who, lacking a little in the internal certainty, or facing an overwhelming social opposition, have descended into futility and failure.

We propose a philosophy and a way of life having a pragmatic appeal to such minds.

A vast number of the human race has the mentality of slaves. Following Barnum, we can also deduce an appropriate number of slave masters.

There is no criticism here. The orders of nature are obvious, and acceptable to the philosophic. But, to the slave mind, there is often something unendurable in the notion of freedom and independence; it would have all men as its brothers in bondage. With this, the slave masters are in full accord.

It would be tedious to examine the techniques by which slavery has been fostered; the superstitious and authoritative devices, religious, political, social and economic, which have forged the chains. Whole philosophies, conceiving the Universe of nature as sorrow, and the nature of man as sin, have been constructed to palliate sacrifice, expiation and obedience.

God and Pope and king, society, humanity, the people, the proletariat, the family, war, the national emergency and all the other bogeys from the armory of fear have been summoned to confront the non-groveler. And those psychological weapons have been terribly enhanced.

This is obvious; and there is room in the world for animal acts and animal trainers—but not more than enough room!

If the individual abdicates his independence in the face of this rabbit hypnosis, this prestidigation, then he has deserved the bondage into which he is delivered.

It is a matter of balance. The leopard won't change his spots—not very rapidly—nor is it needful that he should. It is only needful that the lion take his proper place in the jungle, and keep the leopard and the rabbit where they belong.

The creative individual must take his place as a creative leader in society. He must fulfill his destiny and his responsibility; he can achieve both in fearlessly following his creative Will—his own inner truth; and, in inevitable corollary, he must know and assist others who strive to do likewise.

Then, by leading the slaves a little out of slavery, and the masters a little into humanity and culture—maintaining all the while his own inviolable independence—he will achieve that balance which alone gives significance to the human story.

II

This exposition of the Rights of Man is a statement of first principles. You are referred to Crowley's works, the writings of Nietzsche, Mencken and Bertrand Russell, Emerson's essay on Self-Reliance,[16] and the Declaration of Independence and Bill of Rights in the American Constitution. Here I am not unduly concerned with theory, but rather with you, who, like myself, have independently reached these conclusions, and who are interested in a practical reduction.

Freedom is twofold: there is the freedom within, and the freedom without; and, like all things, the first freedom starts at the home plate.

The mainspring of an individual is his creative Will. This Will is the sum of his tendencies, his destiny, his inner truth. It is one with the force that makes the birds sing and flowers bloom; as inevitable as gravity, as implicit as a bowel movement, it informs alike atoms and men and suns.

To the man who knows this Will, there is no why or why not, no can or cannot; he *IS!*

There is no known force that can turn an apple into an alley cat; there is no known force that can turn a man from his Will. This is the triumph of genius; that, surviving the centuries, enlightens the world.

This force burns in every man.

There are those who are too cowardly, too weak, to seek or express it.

There are those who are too full of pretense, of gullibility, of fear and greed, to give it utterance.

Their lot is bitterness, failure and frustration; dust and ashes are their portion.

There are those who are bewildered, at odds with themselves, overwhelmed by adversity. They seek the light, and if they persevere, they will find it—within Themselves.

---

16. [Ralph Waldo Emerson, "Self-Reliance," in *Essays: First Series* (1841).]

LIBER LXXVII

"the law of
the strong:
this is our law
and the joy
of the world."

—*AL* II:21

"Do what thou wilt shall be the whole of the Law."—*AL* I:40

"thou hast no right but to do thy will. Do that, and no other shall say nay."

—*AL* I:42–3

"Every man and every woman is a star."—*AL* I:3

There is no god but man.

1. Man has the right to live by his own law—
    to live in the way that he wills to do:
    to work as he will:
    to play as he will:
    to rest as he will:
    to die when and how he will.

2. Man has the right to eat what he will:
    to drink what he will:
    to dwell where he will:
    to move as he will on the face of the earth.

3. Man has the right to think what he will:
    to speak what he will:
    to write what he will:
    to draw, paint, carve, etch, mould, build as he will:
    to dress as he will.

4. Man has the right to love as he will:—
    "take your fill and will of love as ye will, when, where, and with whom ye
    will."—*AL* I:51

5. Man has the right to kill those who would thwart these rights.
    "the slaves shall serve."—*AL* II:58

"Love is the law, love under will."—*AL* I:57

III

What are the obstacles to the attainment of the Will? There are many, but they may be grouped into certain primary divisions. And the name of every one of them is FEAR.

1. Fear of Incompetence

"I would like to, but I could never do it."

This is the flimsiest of excuses;—a narcissistic pap poisoning creation at its source. Confidence, enthusiasm, belief and egotism are the roots of creation.

BELIEVE IN YOURSELF.

That is the first rule. Humility can come later. Applaud yourself to yourself. Be proud—you are unique, and marvelously made. There is none other like you.

2. Fear of the Opinion of Others

"What would people say?"

What people? What would they say? To hell with them. Every genius that lighted the world has outraged public opinion. Do you fear that pack of cards?

BE YOURSELF.

Be true to yourself; be honest; enjoy yourself; go your own way, the way of the stars.

3. Fear of Hurting Others

"Mother wouldn't want me to —— ! "

Are you yourself or another? Whose life do you live? To whom are you responsible? Who is your master? Shall we ban cigarettes because they make Mrs. Grundy cough, hang lumber dealers because Christ was crucified, and rend Edison because Johnny was electrocuted?

Does it kill mother when you stay out until one? Is hubby so dreadfully hurt over that flirtation, and wifey in tears about the blonde? This is a subtle device of the slave master: "Do what I say or I'll feel badly."

EXPRESS YOURSELF.

Live your own life—follow your own star. As the Bible has it: "Forsake your father and mother."[17] "Let the dead bury the dead."[18] Let the sick tend the sick. But follow yourself, and no other christ or god. You are sufficient; you justify yourself; you are your own reason:

THERE IS NO MORE NEEDED.

You should be polite about it; you may even be gentle about it. Wanton hurt is needless and gains nothing; but inner, inflexible strength, terribly gentle in its own right of expression, can and *must* follow its own Will as surely as a star follows its own orbit, undeterred and undisturbed by the wailing of inhabitants of minor satellites.

4. Fear of Insecurity

"I might lose my job."

This is the most paltry, the most despicable of the excuses—this slavish whine for daily bread: "Anything you say, masters. I'll be good; just feed me!"

HAVE FORTITUDE.

Be courageous, and the adventure of Life is yours. Failure—can there be an ultimate failure where manhood is sustained? Is not any failure in freedom better than any success in the Slave Pen?

---

17. [Parsons seems to have inverted Ps. 27:10: "When my father and my mother forsake me, then the Lord will take me up," but may have intended Gen. 2:24: "Therefore shall a man leave his father and his mother, and shall cleave unto his wife, and they shall be one flesh," echoed in Eph. 5:31.]

18. [Matt. 8:22.]

"Yes," you might agree—at least I assume that somebody might agree—"but these things are difficult. Where do we start?"

We start, naturally, with the least of the little things. For on the other end of the fulcrum from that little thing is the Universe, and all your heart's desire. Dedicate yourself to your best and highest, and begin. What is the person you most desire to be—I mean, freely and honestly, not morally? Imitate that person, and what began as imitation will end as perfection.

It is possible to cultivate habits of mind and of attention. The splendor of nature is all about us, immortal in loveliness, inexhaustible in wonder. The sky calls us to the high places; the wind and the rain greet us; trees and grasses speak to us, mountains and the great plains and green valleys. We have only to open our minds and hearts to the eternal forces, and we and the eternal forces are one.

From such harmonies the creative Will draws force to inform the mind. He who has opened the way to nature will not wait long to know his own Way.

In the beginning, any consistent action dedicated to the discovery of the Will, or to its development, suffices. The nature of an act is in no wise important, so long as it serves as a lever to set the Will in motion, and so long as it is repeated performed.

Almost any device is permissible if it helps. The use of a talisman, fetish or image symbolizing the Will; the use of a daily formula or ritual; and most especially the dedication of a certain period every day—rain or shine, in sickness or health, in enthusiasm or loathing—for the exclusive practice of the dedicatory act. There is a danger: mind- or muscle-building as an end in itself can degenerate into a subtle form of masturbation.

The Will must be freed of its fetters. The ruthless examination and destruction of taboos, complexes, frustrations, dislikes, fears and disgusts hostile to the Will is essential to progress. Even in the case of pet preferences and prejudices, it must be realized that those things are only significant to the individual; meaningless and often silly in the larger world. On a hot day, Galahad probably stank under his armor. And that sensibility which is nauseated by the sex odor of its own kind, and titillated by the sex odor of plants, might be profitably studied under the heading of a perversion.

Now suppose that the second step is reached. The Will is beginning to flow. You know who you are, what you are; you have discovered your destiny.

It is a time for rejoicing, but not for relaxation. There is no reason in nature why you cannot write music beyond Beethoven, poetry beyond Shelley, out-invent Edison, or out-theorize Einstein!

They are beacons, lighting a sky which you, in your own time and in your own way, will one day illumine.

The task is just begun. There is work ahead—years of work—but work in the real world. Woe to him who dallies with escapist daydreams, with fancies and visions and trances, with specious words and poses, and the onanistic flattery of his fellow opium eaters.

The Will is creative and dynamic, and it must create and move in hard fact. By their fruits shall ye known them. "Success is your proof"[19] —but YOUR success, on your own terms. The way is hard; you will face failure after failure, fall after fall. But each fall and each failure is a success, a new jewel for the diadem of conscious experience.

Life—beautiful, terrible, splendid and pitiless; life is your adversary and your love. She you must accept unreservedly, and she you must overcome. She woos to destroy; she submits to conquer; she conquers to submit. That Tigress is your paramour; the Cosmos is your adventure.

And the goal? The totality of experience—the gesture commensurate with the Universe.

Is that not enough?

---

19. [*Liber AL vel Legis, The Book of the Law* III:46.]